MANY ARE CALLED
BUT FEW ARE CHOSEN

H. VERLAN ANDERSEN

ISBN: 1540449203
ISBN-13: 978-1540449207

Special edition printing by The Ezra Taft Benson Society
ezrataftbensonsociety.org

CONTENTS

INTRODUCTORY COMMENT

It is unusual to find in recorded history a nation of people who enjoyed the privilege of self-government. It is even more of a rarity to find a nation which possessed this privilege along with the gospel of Christ. This unique combination of blessings was given to the Nephites just 125 years before the resurrected Christ visited them in 34 A.D. However, by the time Christ appeared, the Nephites had destroyed their government by the voice of the people.

In this dispensation, the people of this nation have been made beneficiaries of this same incomparable set of privileges. There is extensive evidence that we are in the process of destroying the government God has given us (as did the Nephites).

The scriptures indicate that when the Lord gives to a people both a knowledge of the gospel and the power of self-government, He also places upon them responsibilities of great magnitude with respect to their government. The gospel teachings provide an understanding of the proper function of government which lays an extremely important political duty upon those who have these teachings. While we may try to separate this duty from our religious obligations, a close examination of the central problem of government reveals it to be essentially moral or religious in nature.

The power to participate in the governing process is the power to determine under what circumstances it is legal to use force on our fellow men. Governments exist for only one purpose: to make and enforce rules governing human conduct. Every rule or law which is passed has attached to it a penalty. The penalty invariably takes from the disobedient either his life, his liberty, or his property.

Under a government subject to the voice of the people, the ultimate responsibility for laws, and therefore for determining when it is proper to kill a person, jail him, or take from him his property, rests directly on the voting citizen. There is no other place to rest the credit or blame for what is done in the name of government.

This is a moral question of the most serious nature and for that very reason, it is also religious. Thus, the central problem of government, is a religious one, and anyone who assumes that he can form his political beliefs without consulting his ethics, which have their basis in religious conviction, is deceiving himself either about the true nature of government, or his moral responsibility for its actions.

The problem of government is also of interest to Latter-day Saints in connection with the privilege of holding the Priesthood. When we act through government, we are using physical coercion to compel our fellow men to do as we say, or forfeit their lives, liberties, or properties. It should be immediately apparent that we might direct our agent, the government, to use compulsion for wrong purposes, as well as for those which are right. If we do abuse the power of government, who will deny that this constitutes an exercise of unrighteous dominion?

Doctrine and Covenants Section 121 tells us, in effect, that if we exercise control, dominion, or compulsion in any degree of unrighteousness, and fail to mend our ways, amen to our priesthood. Thus, it is possible that we priesthood bearers are jeopardizing our callings by abusing the rare privilege of self-government.

The danger that we will abuse the police power any time that it is made subject to our direction is most likely for several reasons:

1. It is the nature and disposition of almost all men, as soon as they get a little authority, as they suppose, they will immediately begin to exercise unrighteous dominion. (D&C 121:39)
2. When we use force upon each other through government, we do so without fear of retaliation or condemnation, so conscience alone remains to restrain us.
3. We are easily deceived about government, because we are inclined to accept the following fallacies:
   (a) Anything legal is also moral.
   (b) We are not individually responsible for government action.

(c) A different moral law applies when men act in concert, than it does when they act alone.

Latter-day Saint scriptures indicate that it was necessary for the Lord to set this nation up as a free people before He could restore the gospel to earth. (3 Ne. 21:4) They also tell us that the Lord caused our Constitutional form of government to be established so that men could exercise moral agency. (D&C 101:77-78) To enable the Church to continue to exist, and to permit men to continue to exercise their agency in this land, it is essential that this government of freedom be preserved. For these reasons, if for no others, the Lord is deeply concerned about our political institutions and beliefs.

It is not surprising therefore, that the Lord has given us extensive instructions on matters of government. It is the hope of the author that those who read this material may find, as I have, that the words of God's prophets, together with the United States Constitution, which He caused to be established, provide complete guidance on all important political problems.

If this is true, there is no reason why those who accept the words of the prophets, may not come to a unity of political belief, and thus put an end to that spirit of contention, which, if not checked, may produce serious consequences among us. President McKay has expressed the hope that this will occur. Said he:

> Next to being one in worshipping God, there is nothing in this world upon which this Church should be more united than upholding and defending the Constitution of the United States. (*Statements on Communism and the Constitution of the United States.* Deseret Book Co., 1966 p. 6)

Of course I believe in following the prophets. I just think they ought to keep their mouths shut about socialism, government subsidies to the poor, government subsidies to businesses, government schools, licensing, free agency, etc. (A common fallacy you may have heard before)

CHAPTER I

THE PROBLEM

The title of this work, *Many Are Called But Few Are Chosen*, is a quotation from the Doctrine and Covenants, a modern day scripture of the Church of Jesus Christ of Latter-day Saints. This statement appears several times in that volume and in each case where it is found, that group referred to as the many who are called, are those who hold the Priesthood in the Church. It is from this body of men that only a *few will be chosen.*

What does the scripture mean by this assertion? Is the Lord warning us that only a few who hold the priesthood here will be permitted to exercise this power in the hereafter? Is this what is meant by not being *chosen?* Are we also to conclude that only a few of these priesthood bearers will inherit the highest degree of glory which is reserved for those who exercise the Melchizedek Priesthood?

If these questions are answered in the affirmative, what causes this large body of men to forfeit that power which is more precious to them than life itself? Why aren't more priesthood bearers aware that this, one of the greatest tragedies imaginable, is taking place? Is the answer to be found in those scriptural statements which tell us that the many who are not chosen, are *walking in darkness at noon-day?* (D&C 95:6) Are we failing to learn that lesson which governs the exercise of these powers in heaven? (D&C 121:34-36)

Are we aware that almost all of us are inclined to exercise unrighteous dominion, and this is the reason only a few will be chosen? (D&C 121:39-40) If it be a fact that almost all of us are using unrighteous compulsion upon each other, what is the activity which

6

condemns us? Do we realize that if a man continues to exercise control, dominion, or compulsion upon another in any degree of unrighteousness, that it will be *Amen to the priesthood or the authority of that man?* (D&C 121:37)

The following discussion undertakes to answer the above questions, and to develop these themes:

1. The ultimate in joy and freedom which men seek consists of the power of the Priesthood and opportunity to use that power to increase freedom.
2. This power and opportunity will be denied to us to the same extent that we fail to overcome the almost universal disposition to destroy freedom by exercising unrighteous dominion.

It is also the purpose of this discussion to analyze freedom by breaking it down into its component parts and then indicating what men must do and what they must not do through the agency of government, to preserve these elements of freedom.

The one great problem of intelligent man which encompasses all others is to discover and obey those laws which will make him free because joy, the object of existence, can be measured by the amount of freedom man has. Men establish governments for the purpose of securing freedom, but in doing so they create the greatest threat to freedom which exists—the government under which they live. This same agency which is so necessary to secure freedom may also become its greatest enemy. Thus it becomes imperative that governments be kept within their proper bounds if freedom is to be maintained.

Men can exercise freedom only if they possess the following:

(1) life, (2) liberty (the absence of restraint), (3) property, and (4) knowledge.

When men become wicked, they act to destroy these necessary elements rather than preserve them, and freedom becomes impossible to maintain no matter what the form of government. There is an inexorable law of nature in operation which decrees that no man can act with the purpose of destroying another's freedom without losing

7

his own. The operation of this divine law of retribution is easily observed in a society of self-governing people.

Selfish, needful man is restrained from forcibly taking the life, liberty or property of his neighbor by these considerations:

(1) conscience, (2) fear of retaliation (3) fear of condemnation of others.

When men act through government, they do so without fear of retaliation or condemnation, and conscience alone remains to curb the propensity to abuse power.

Therefore, when a nation of people who have had the power of government placed in their hands become evil and without conscience, they will use that power to plunder and enslave one another until freedom is destroyed. It is a truism taught by the sages and prophets and proved repeatedly in the history of nations that wickedness and liberty cannot exist side by side.

Equally fatal to freedom is the ignorance or indifference of the voting majority. Unless they perceive with clarity that line which divides right from wrong in government action, and resist with firmness any attempt to cross it, the natural tendency of men to abuse power will cause those in office to enlarge their functions until liberty is crushed under the weight of bureaucratic despotism.

Therefore a nation must not only remain moral to remain free, but it must also be alert and informed. Furthermore the people must have a standard by which to distinguish with precision those functions which preserve freedom from those which destroy it. The standard which is used must be widely known, universally acceptable to moral people, and easily applied.

It is one of the main objects of this work to point out that the only standard which fills these requirements is the Lord's Golden Rule. He has decreed this to be the law and the prophets. (Matt. 7:12; 3 Ne. 14:12) The Golden Rule is the only moral standard upon which agreement can be reached. Conscience is the one test everyone can and should use to determine the propriety of every use of force through government. (D&C 134:2-5, Alma 30:7-11)

WILFORD WOODRUFF

You may wish to know why I make these remarks. I will tell you. Because God himself grants this right to every human being upon the earth irrespective of race or color; it is part of the divine economy not to force any man to heaven, not to coerce the mind but to leave it free to act for itself.

He lays before His creature man the everlasting Gospel, the principles of life and salvation, and then leaves him to choose for himself or to reject for himself, with the definite understanding that he becomes responsible to Him for the results of his acts. (Wilford Woodruff, *Journal of Discourses*, Vol. 23, p. 77)

LORENZO SNOW

In things that pertain to celestial glory there can be no forced operations. We must do according as the spirit of the Lord operates upon our understandings and feelings. We cannot be crowded into matters, however great might be the blessing attending such procedure. We cannot be forced into living a celestial law; we must do this ourselves, of our own free will. And whatever we do in regard to the principle of the United Order, we must do it because we desire to do it....

The United Order is not French Communism. (Lorenzo Snow, *Journal of Discourses*, Vol. 19, p.346, 349-350)

JOSEPH F. SMITH

...We must choose righteous men, good men to fill these positions. Hence if you will only get good men to fill these offices no one should care who they are, so that you have agreed upon them, and were one. We want you to be one both in temporal, political and religious things, in fact, in everything you put your hands to in righteousness. We want you to be one, one as God and Christ are one, seeing eye to eye. Do not try to crush anybody, or build yourselves up at the expense of you neighbor. Do not do it; it is a custom of the world, and it is a wrong principle. (Joseph F. Smith, *Journal of Discourses*, Vol. 25, p. 251)

CHAPTER II

FREEDOM—ITS ULTIMATE MEANING

In a statement contained in the Book of John 8:31-32, Christ promised His disciples freedom if they learned the truth and followed His teachings. Said He:

> If ye continue in my word, then are ye my disciples indeed; And ye shall know the truth, and the truth shall make you free.

From this, it would appear that only those who obey Christ's teachings (*continue in my word*) shall know the truth and be free. The promise of freedom to those who will obey, runs throughout all scripture. Conversely, we are warned that if we are wicked, our enslavement by Satan is certain. Father Lehi told us:

> Wherefore, men are free according to the flesh; and all things are given them which are expedient unto man. And they are free to choose liberty and eternal life, through the great mediation of all men, or to choose captivity and death, according to the captivity and power of the devil; for he seeketh that all men might be miserable like unto himself. (2 Nephi 2:27)

There is a relationship between righteousness and freedom on the one hand, and evil and a denial of freedom on the other, which

10

allows us to define good and evil strictly in terms of whether the act in question increases or decreases freedom. Both the laws of God and the laws of civilized man have always defined good as that which increases and preserves freedom. Evil constitutes its destruction or decrease. The essential truth of this proposition will be more readily apparent if we identify each of the elements of freedom, and note those acts which have the effect of preserving or destroying these elements.

Freedom can be defined as the power and opportunity to accomplish our goals. An element of freedom is some possession which enables us to do this. Those components or elements of freedom, which we must possess, in order to accomplish our purposes, are:

(1) life, (2) liberty, (3) property, and (4) knowledge.

Let us consider each of these elements and note the immoral nature of those acts which destroy them, and the moral nature of those acts which supply, or preserve them.

LIFE

The most obvious requirement for a person to accomplish his purposes is some degree of physical and mental health and strength, or life itself. Throughout history, the destruction or injury of this element of freedom by murder, mayhem, or assault and battery, has been a sin in the sight of God and a crime in the eyes of the law. Prostitution of the God-given power of pro-creation is also regarded as criminal and evil.

Conversely, whenever we act to preserve the life of another, or when parents provide bodies for children, supply them with a home, and raise them to maturity, they are fulfilling God's commandments to be good Samaritans, and to multiply and replenish the earth. Thus, that which provides this element is called good; that which destroys it is labelled bad.

LIBERTY

The second element, liberty, is the absence of coercion or restraint. When we enslave a fellow man, or unjustly subject him to our will, we have committed both a sin and a crime. The Lord has said:

> Therefore, it is not right that any man should be in bondage one to another. And for this purpose have I established the Constitution of this land, by the hands of wise men whom I raised up unto this very purpose, and redeemed the land by the shedding of blood. (D&C 101:79-80)

In this passage, the Lord not only condemns slavery, but also speaks His approval of those who act to liberate the captive and establish a government prohibiting bondage.

PROPERTY

The third element is the right and control of property. Wealth, or organized raw materials, is an essential ingredient of freedom: First, because our very survival depends upon access to such things as food, clothing, and shelter; secondly, because the right and control of property permits us to increase our physical and mental powers almost without limit. By utilizing tools, machinery, equipment, and harnessing electrical, nuclear, and other forms of energy, our ability to achieve our purposes is raised to the *n*th power.

If you deny a person access to the necessities of life, of course he will die. If you deny him these necessities unless he does what you say, you can make him your slave because most of us will obey nearly any command to remain alive. As Alexander Hamilton has said:

> A power over a man's subsistence amounts to a power over his will. (*Federalist Papers* No. 79)

The right to own and control property or wealth is as essential to the exercise of freedom as life itself and must be protected or individual liberty is impossible.

We all come into this life owning the same—nothing. All we ever legally own is what we earn or receive as a gift. As children, we are quite dependent upon our parents to even stay alive. If the right and control of property is protected, we may, as we grow to maturity, use the health and strength of our mind and body and take of the unlimited raw materials and energy about us and fashion these into consumable products. We may either use these products ourselves or exchange them for the goods and services of our fellow men and thus free ourselves from dependence upon others. If we are willing to labor hard enough and restrain our desire to consume, we can make ourselves what is called independently wealthy.

The Lord has told us there is plenty for all. He has been over-generous in making available the raw materials and energy of this earth for the very purpose that we may exercise our agency. This is indicated in the following scripture:

> For the earth is full, and there is enough and to spare; yea,
> I prepared all things, and have given unto the children of men
> to be agents unto themselves. (D&C 104:17)

It is clear that the right and control of property is a basic element of freedom. It is as vital as life and liberty, neither of which are of any value without it.

When we deprive another of this element by stealing, destroying, or otherwise denying him the right to control what he owns, we have to this same extent diminished his freedom and violated the laws of God and man. On the other hand, when we use the strength of our minds and bodies to organize wealth and provide ourselves and others with the necessities of life, or the means of achieving life's goals, we are obeying God's commandments to work and be charitable with what we produce.

KNOWLEDGE

The fourth element of freedom mentioned is knowledge. One may achieve a desired result only by complying with that particular law upon which the result depends. No person can consciously obey a law unless he knows what that law is. Thus, freedom to attain any goal is impossible without a knowledge of the pertinent facts and laws.

If one bases his actions upon false information and principles, his failure is certain, his efforts rendered futile, and the exercise of freedom frustrated. Consequently, one who deceives or deliberately

13

misleads, is condemned by both the laws of God and man. The effect of perverting the truth hinders or prevents compliance with law and destroys freedom.

In contrast, one of the most approved and righteous of all callings is to increase freedom by disseminating truth, thereby increasing men's ability to reach their goals.

FREEDOM—THE POWER TO AFFECT FREEDOM

It will be noted that substantially all deeds which are considered evil are included among those actions which destroy the elements of freedom. Conversely, substantially all actions regarded as righteous have the effect of providing or increasing these same elements. If we include in our definition the motives which cause men to preserve the elements of freedom on the one hand, and to destroy them on the other, we have comprehended essentially all which is either good or evil in life.

In the following quotation President David O. McKay expresses his belief that good and evil can be completely defined in terms of free agency:

> I refer to the fundamental principle of the gospel, free agency. References in the scriptures show that this principle is (1) essential to man's salvation; and (2) may become a measuring rod by which the actions of men, of organizations of nations may be judged. (*Gospel Ideals*, pp. 299-300)

We may use freedom as a standard by which all actions may be judged because joy, the ultimate purpose of existence, may be measured in terms of the amount of freedom one has. Freedom is the one indispensable element of joy, and the relationship between them is such that it can be stated as a law that joy is a function of freedom, and varies directly therewith. It is also true that misery is an inevitable consequence of slavery. No intelligent person can be convinced to the contrary.

We have heretofore defined freedom as the power and opportunity to achieve goals. Let us observe in the light of the above discussion that the only goals which are of any importance are to increase or decrease joy and freedom. In other words, the only desires which matter are to do good or evil, and these desires are nothing more nor less than the desire to increase or destroy joy and freedom. This being so, we may now restate our definition of freedom as follows:

Freedom is the power and opportunity to affect the freedom of others.

We have all been taught the doctrine of personal free agency and that no individual is ever compelled by force or other means to comply with divine edicts and philosophy. We have been informed that a long time ago in the pre-existence there was a rebellion in heaven, and because one notable character, who had been entrusted with great authority, rebelled and led many away with him, he had to be cast out of the kingdom. However we should remember that every principle and law existing in the celestial kingdom has been proved to be perfect through the eternities through which they have come. If any individual proves himself worthy for the exaltation in that kingdom, it will be by strict obedience to every principle and covenant here existing. Therefore we may be assured that every law and principle thereunto pertaining is perfect and cannot be amended or discarded because of its perfection. (Joseph Fielding Smith, *Answers to Gospel Questions,* Vol. 4 p. 69)

The modern trend of the nations is towards dictatorship. It is taking form in two great camps, but, nevertheless, the direction is the same, although it is being reached by different routes. On the one side the direction to make an end of all nations, is through communism... (Joseph Fielding Smith, *The Progress of Man,* p. 397)

CHAPTER III

THE DIVINE LAW OF RESTORATION

By defining freedom as the power and opportunity to affect the freedom of others, we are able to see the necessity of the existence of that fundamental law of intelligent existence which decrees that those who would deny freedom to others shall lose their own, and those who seek to increase the freedom of others shall have their own increased.

The punitive side of this law was recognized by Abraham Lincoln in the following statement.

> Those who deny freedom to others deserve it not for themselves, and under a just God, cannot long retain it.

The complete statement of the law was given by Christ in the Sermon on the Mount:

> For with what judgment ye judge, ye shall be judged; and with what measure ye mete, it shall be measured to you again. (Matt. 7:2; 3 Ne. 14:2. {See also D&C 1:10})

The prophet Alma explained this divine law of restoration to his son, Corianton, in some detail. Let us consider some of his words:

> And it is requisite with the justice of God that men should be judged according to their works; and if their works

were good in this life, and the desires of their hearts were good, that they should also, at the last day, be restored unto that which is good. And if their works are evil they shall be restored unto them for evil...the meaning of the word restoration is to bring back again evil for evil, or carnal for carnal, or devilish for devilish—good for that which is good; righteous for that which is righteous; just for that which is just; merciful for that which is merciful.... For that which ye do send out shall return unto you again, and be restored; therefore, the word restoration more fully condemneth the sinner, and justifieth him not at all. (Alma 41:3, 4, 13, 15)

Why is it that the justice of God demands that those who have committed evil must have evil restored to them? Or, defining evil as the destruction of freedom, why is it that those who have undertaken to destroy the freedom of others must lose their own? Is this merely an act of divine revenge, or is there some fundamental reason which requires the execution of this law?

Let us first consider the problem from the viewpoint of those who would be the victims. If those who desire to use their freedom to destroy the freedom of others were to have their powers and opportunities to do so continually increased, then joy, the object of existence, would be unattainable. In its place misery would prevail because, as we have seen above, the denial of freedom is the very essence of unhappiness.

Now let us consider the matter from the viewpoint of those who are punished with a loss of their freedom. Are their interests best served by having their freedom taken from them? Or must we conclude that the interests of men are basically antagonistic so that the evil-doer must be harmed to prevent unjust suffering by those whose freedom he would destroy?

In trying to answer this question, let us first recall that we have defined evil as the motivating force which causes people to destroy freedom. But those motivated by evil are themselves miserable. No one has ever seen a person motivated exclusively by hate, envy, lust, etc. who was happy. The more intense the hate and the desire to destroy others, the greater the misery. *Wickedness never was happiness.* (Alma 41:10) For the good of such a person, his capacity to destroy freedom should be decreased.

Thus it is seen that men's interests are harmonious. It is for the benefit of everyone concerned that those who seek to destroy freedom shall have their power and opportunity to do so diminished. Furthermore, where repentance is possible, there is an additional reason for taking freedom from those who abuse it. The loss of any of the elements of freedom is painful to bear and one who is called upon to suffer such a loss may come to recognize the error of his ways and repent of his evil desires.

In contrast to that part of the law of restoration which requires a diminution of the freedom of the evil doer, let us observe the operation of the law on behalf of those who work only righteousness. One who would act only to increase freedom may safely have his powers to do so increased without limit.

Having in mind the divine law of restoration, let us re-examine the definition of good and evil given above which labels as evil acts which destroy the elements of freedom, and as good, those acts which provide or protect them. It is immediately apparent that such a definition is incomplete as it stands. Someone must enforce the law of retribution and, in doing so, must destroy the elements of freedom in the process. To preserve freedom it is imperative that those who act with the purpose of destroying it should have their power and opportunity to do so curtailed. Thus, it is justifiable and proper to destroy another's freedom under this circumstance—to execute the law of retribution.

In commanding man to utilize the police power to punish criminals, the Lord directed him to learn His law of justice and co-operate with Him in executing it here on earth. When a person breaks a criminal law by destroying life, liberty, property, or knowledge, the Lord wants us to punish such a person by depriving him of one or more of these elements of freedom.

If we destroy these elements for any other reason, the law of retribution operates on us to cause a loss of our own freedom. This, then, is the answer to the great problem of government: under what circumstances does a group have the moral right to deprive their fellow man of his life, liberty, or property?

We desire to more fully discuss the Lord's answer to this question but before doing so, let us take a more comprehensive view of the operation of the law of retribution. Let us note its enforcement in both the pre-mortal and the post-mortal life, as it applies to the right to exercise the power of the Priesthood.

THE DIVINE LAW OF RETRIBUTION AND THE EXERCISE OF PRIESTHOOD POWER

In the pre-earth life, God offered His children His divine power, the Priesthood. (Alma 13:3-4). This power has been described by President Brigham Young in these words:

> The Priesthood of the Son of God is the law by which the worlds are, were and will continue forever and ever. It is that system which brings worlds into existence and peoples them, gives them their seasons and times by which they...go into a higher state of existence. (John A. Widstoe, *Priesthood and Church Government*, p. 33, Deseret Book Co. 1939).

One in full possession of such a power would be able to accomplish any and every righteous desire. He would have complete and absolute freedom. No one can imagine greater power and freedom than this. It is the supreme power of the universe.

Some to whom this power was offered in the pre-earth life used it for proper purposes, and were permitted to continue to exercise it here. Others sought to abuse it and lost it. It appears that Satan was one of those to whom God offered His power for we are told he was:

> An angel of God, who was in authority in the presence of God. (D&C 76:25)

However, because he...sought to destroy the agency of man, which I, the Lord God, had given him, and also, that I should give unto him mine own power; by the power of mine Only Begotten, I caused that he should be cast down. (Moses 4:3)

God's authority was thus denied Satan and the one-third of the hosts of heaven who followed him because of their desire to destroy free agency. They were also separated from the other two-thirds whose freedom they sought to destroy. Of course, they are here on earth as spirits, enticing man to murder, to enslave, to steal and otherwise destroy freedom, but they are powerless to do these things themselves. Neither can they have children, organize the earth's raw materials, or otherwise increase freedom. This is the first instance of which we have record where the Lord's divine law of retribution was made effective.

Though the other two-thirds of God's children rejected the doctrine of compulsion and elected to follow Christ, the danger that we will even yet subject ourselves to the penalty of the law of retribution is extremely great, because the scriptures tell us:

> We have learned by sad experience that it is the nature and disposition of almost all men, as soon as they get a little authority, as they suppose, they will immediately begin to exercise unrighteous dominion. (D&C 121:39)

From this we learn that almost all men are still afflicted with a tendency to destroy one another's freedom. Unless we overcome this weakness, it is inevitable that the Lord will find it necessary to withhold from us His power for the simple reason that we cannot be relied upon to use it exclusively for righteous purposes.

It is observed that Latter-day Saint doctrine teaches that there are three degrees of glory in the hereafter with subdivisions within these different degrees and that man, if he lives worthy, may inherit the highest, or celestial degree where God and Christ dwell. But our doctrine also teaches that relatively few Church members will merit such an exalted state. Christ told both the Jews and the Nephites that but few of them would enter in at the strait gate. (Matt. 7:13, 14; 3 Ne. 14:13, 14). A similar warning has been issued to members of His Church in these latter days:

> Verily, verily, I say unto you, except ye abide my law ye cannot attain to this (the highest) glory. for strait is the gate, and narrow the way that leadeth unto the exaltation and continuation of the lives, and few there be that find it, because ye receive me not in the world neither do ye know me. (D&C 132:21-22)

21

If it be true, as appears to be the case, that the group to which this revelation is addressed are the members of the Church of Jesus Christ of Latter-day Saints, it is certain that only a *few* of this membership will prove worthy of *exaltation and continuation of lives.*

Perhaps the most explicit confirmation of the fact that only a few of the members of Christ's Church will inherit the highest degree of glory, is provided by those scriptures which discuss the fate of the majority of those who hold the Priesthood and the requirement that those who enter that highest degree be worthy to exercise this power.

Doctrine and Covenants 76:56-57 states that those who inherit the highest glory will hold the Melchizedek Priesthood. However, certain other revelations seem to declare that only a *few* of the many upon whom such Priesthood is conferred in this life will be chosen to continue in their callings in the next. If this be true, then the *many* will not only forfeit their rights to the Priesthood, but to a place in this highest degree of glory as well.

Those scriptural statements which most fully discuss the condemnation of the majority of the priesthood are found in D&C, Sec. 121.

This section says not just once, but twice that *many are called but few are chosen.* In each case, the passages are referring to those who hold the Priesthood. Does this mean that the great majority of those upon whom the Priesthood is conferred in this life will have it taken from them in the next? Is this what is meant by not being chosen?

It is difficult to place any other interpretation upon the language used. It is incontestable that the Lord in speaking of the *many who are called* is referring to bearers of the Priesthood. It is from this body of men that only a few will be chosen.

There is this much which is certain about the statement: the many are going to be denied some privilege or blessing which only the *few* will enjoy. That this privilege is the right to hold the Priesthood seems to be indicated by other verses in this section.

Verse 37 states that even though the rights of the Priesthood may be conferred upon one, he may lose them again. The words which state that a man's Priesthood may terminate are these: *Amen to the Priesthood or the authority of that man.* One of the ways in which one may lose his power is by using compulsion unrighteously upon his fellow men. Part of verse 37 reads as follows:

When we undertake to…exercise control, dominion or compulsion upon the souls of the children of men, in any degree of unrighteousness…Amen to the priesthood or the authority of that man.

Then verse 39 tells us that almost all men have a disposition which causes them to do this very thing. The conclusion drawn in verse 40— *Hence many are called but few are chosen*—seems to have only one meaning; amen to the priesthood of almost all men.

Verse 36 supports this interpretation. It says that the rights of the Priesthood are inseparably connected with the powers of heaven and that the powers of heaven cannot be handled only upon principles of righteousness.

Thus, while we are permitted to exercise the Priesthood here on earth, though still afflicted with a weakness to abuse authority, the *powers of heaven* and the Priesthood which is inseparably connected therewith, cannot be controlled by one with such a disposition.

If, at the end of this life, we are still inclined to exercise unrighteous dominion and thereby deny others that freedom to which they are entitled, the divine law of retribution will demand that our power and opportunity to affect the freedom of others be restricted. The Lord will have no alternative but to assign us a place in the hereafter with that great majority who cannot be trusted to use authority only for the increase of freedom. God's power cannot be used to defeat God's purposes.

It may seem strange that although we have made a decision in favor of freedom and against compulsion in the pre-earth life, we should be called upon to make it once again. The reason is, of course, that almost all of us are still disposed to exercise unrighteous dominion. By our decision there we gave ourselves a second chance to completely overcome this satanic tendency.

But the only way we can do this, it seems, is to be subjected to Satan's teachings once again. This time, however, we must make our choice under different conditions. Having been rejected by us once, Satan must present his plan in this world in disguise and under circumstances where our physical appetites and desires tempt us to accept and believe it. We must walk by faith and experience a trial of that faith. Only with such tests facing us is it possible to completely reject his philosophy and rid ourselves of this weakness.

SPENCER W. KIMBALL

...Assume that you become the world leader of Socialism and in it have marked success, but through your devotion to it you fail to live the gospel. Where are you then? Is anything worthwhile which will estrange you from your friends, your Church membership, your family, your eternal promises, your faith? You might say that such estrangement is not necessarily a result of your political views, but truthfully hasn't your overpowering interest in your present views already started driving a wedge? (Spencer W. Kimball, *Teachings*, pp. 408-409)

HOWARD W. HUNTER

...We know from both ancient and modern revelation that Satan wished to deny us our independence and agency in that now forgotten moment long ago, even as he wishes to deny them this very hour. Indeed, Satan violently opposed the freedom of choice offered by the Father, so violently that John in the Revelation described "war in heaven" over the matter. (Rev.12:7) Satan would have coerced us, and he would have robbed us of that most precious of gifts if he could: our freedom to choose a divine future and the exaltation we all hope to obtain...

To fully understand this gift of agency and its inestimable worth, it is imperative that we understand that God's chief way of acting is by persuasion and patience and long-suffering, not by coercion and stark confrontation... (Howard W. Hunter, *That We Might Have Joy*, pp. 77-78)

CHAPTER IV

FORFEITURE OF PRIESTHOOD BY DECEPTION

The Lord has told us that Satan's mission here on earth is to win us over by deception:

> And he became Satan, yea, even the devil, the father of all lies, to deceive and to blind men, and to lead them captive at his will, even as many as would not hearken unto my voice. (Moses 4:4)

We have also been warned that Satan would be very successful in his effort to deceive men:

> Behold, here is the agency of man, and here is the condemnation of man; because that which was from the beginning is plainly manifest unto them, and they receive not the light. And every man whose spirit receiveth not the light is under condemnation. And that wicked one cometh and taketh away light and truth, through disobedience, from the children of men, and because of the tradition of their fathers. (D&C 93:31-32, 39)

It is apparent from this passage that Satan is effective among those of us who have truths plainly manifest unto us. It is the Latter-day Saints who have the plain light of the gospel. We are the ones who have much to fear because it is blindness and inability to learn the laws governing the exercise of the Priesthood, coupled with our disposition to exercise unrighteous dominion, which condemn us and cause us to lose our callings. The following two scriptures indicate that this is so:

> But behold, verily I say unto you, that there are many who have been ordained among you, whom I have called but few of them are chosen. They who are not chosen have sinned a very grievous sin, in that they are walking in darkness at noonday. (D&C 95:5-6)

> And why are they not chosen? Because...they do not learn this one lesson—That the rights of the priesthood are inseparably connected with the powers of heaven, and that the powers of heaven cannot be controlled nor handled only upon the principles of righteousness. (D&C 121:34-36)

Perhaps if we were not blind to the fact that we are exercising unrighteous dominion we would repent. Any person who has even a meager understanding of the Priesthood would give all that he possesses to avoid losing it. But having been deceived by Satan, we cannot recognize within ourselves the disposition to abuse authority. Being unaware of the danger we take no steps to avoid it. We are in the position of not being able to repent because we are unconscious of the fact that we are sinning.

It appears that no matter how honorable and well intentioned we may be, if we permit ourselves to be deceived, we will fall short of the Celestial Kingdom. Doctrine and Covenants Section 76 in describing those groups of men who will inherit the intermediate, or Terrestrial Kingdom, mentions the following:

> These are they who are honorable men of the earth, who were blinded by the craftiness of men. (D&C 76:75)

Some may question the justice of a law which denies blessings to one who has lived honorably according to his beliefs but who has been misled by false teachings. We must recognize, however, that no one can possibly receive a blessing unless he has obeyed that law upon which the blessing is predicated. (D&C 130:21) If one is ignorant of the law in question or misconstrues its meaning, he will never become entitled to that blessing.

The scriptures assure us that God will do no injustice to any man. We must conclude therefore, that if an honorable person has been deceived, he has failed in some way. Either he has not sought for the truth diligently enough or he has not searched in the right place.

The prophet, Nephi, in prophesying concerning our day was led to make the following comment:

> And now I, Nephi, cannot say more; the Spirit stoppeth mine utterance, and I am left to mourn because of the unbelief, and the wickedness, and the ignorance, and the stiffneckedness of men; for they will not search knowledge, nor understand great knowledge, when it is given unto them is plainness, even as plain as word can be. (2 Nephi 32:7)

Latter-day Saints might well consider the possibility that we are the ones Nephi was referring to here. There can be no question but that we have been given great knowledge in all plainness. Are we guilty of failing to search and understand what has been given us? And if we are, is it not certain that we will be blinded by the craftiness of men? On the other hand we have been given this promise by the Lord:

> And whoso treasureth up my word, shall not be deceived. (Joseph Smith 1:37 {P. of G. P.})

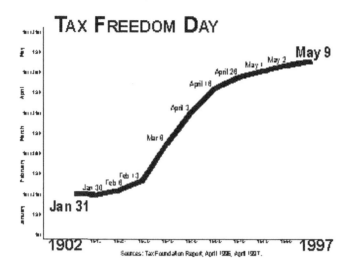

TAX FREEDOM DAY

May 9

May 2

May 1

April 26

April 18

April 3

Mar 8

Feb 13

Feb 8

Jan 30

Jan 31

1902   1997

Sources: Tax Foundation Report, April 1996, April 1997.

How long do you work each year to pay your city, county, state and federal taxes? Since 1930 the increasing burden has been, on average, 1.27 days per year. Your individual stewardship of your individual income declines as soul destroying, government programs expand. What do prophets think of this?

During the first half of the twentieth century we have traveled far into the soul-destroying land of socialism....(David O. McKay, *Gospel Ideals, p. 273)*

We have accepted a frightening degree of socialism in our country. The question is, how much? The amount of freedom depends upon the amount of federal control and spending. A good measurement is to determine the amount, or percentage of income of people that is taken over and spent by the state. ...They now advocate throughout our economy that we "redistribute wealth and income," a good definition of socialism. (Ezra Taft Benson, *This Nation Shall Endure*, p. 114)

I warn you that government subsidies are not the Lord's way; and if we begin to accept, we are on our way to becoming subsidized politically as well as financially. (Harold B. Lee, *The Teachings of Harold B. Lee*, p. 314-315)

CHAPTER V

THE EXERCISE OF UNRIGHTEOUS DOMINION BY ABUSE OF THE POLICE POWER

It may come as a severe shock to priesthood bearers that the majority of us are being deceived, and are so lacking in knowledge of the laws governing the exercise of our powers that we will lose our callings in the hereafter. What is the reason for this walking in darkness at noonday—this inability to see that which is so plainly manifest? D&C 121:34 assigns two reasons for our failure to learn:

(1) We set our hearts so much upon the things of this world.
(2) We aspire to the honor of men.

In summary, then, this is our problem: We forfeit our callings because we fail to overcome the tendency to exercise unrighteous dominion; we do not overcome this tendency because we are blind to the fact that we have such a disposition; our blindness is caused by our pride and an excessive desire for wealth and the honors of men.

Where, in the activities of this life, do priesthood bearers exhibit such an intense desire for the things of this world that we can be deceived into using unrighteous dominion to acquire them? Wherein do we blindly adopt Satan's plan and employ compulsion upon one another? The scriptures are clear that the use of unrighteous dominion is the essence of our sin. The three words—*control*, *dominion*, and *compulsion* used in verse 39 of section 121 to describe the forbidden conduct, all mean the use of restraint or coercion. For example the word *compulsion* is defined by the dictionary as: *An act of compelling, or state of being compelled: subjection to force.*

When one thinks of a person who would stoop to the use of force to acquire wealth or power, he thinks of a criminal. Priesthood bearers are not criminals—at least in the eyes of the law; but are we in the sight of God? Surely a just God would not condemn us for using compulsion unless we actually commit the offense.

One looks in vain for any extensive use of direct force by the ordinary citizen against his neighbor. Do we need to use force ourselves to be held liable? Suppose we get our agent to give us an undeserved position of prominence by using force on our behalf. Would we not be equally guilty?

Every priesthood member belongs to an organization which exercises force on his behalf. What is this organization? It is the government under which he lives. While this force of government is essential for the preservation of freedom, it may also be used to destroy it. Has the Lord provided us with an opportunity to overcome our prevailing dispositions to use force when He placed us under a government subject to the voice of the people? Is this the force we are abusing? Is this where Satan is so highly successful in deceiving us into using his plan of compulsion?

The opportunity for deception is excellent here because there is much confusion and violent disagreement about what the police power should be used for. Some of us are bound to be wrong, and it is entirely possible that most of us are.

Some people may never have considered the possibility that an individual citizen could be morally responsible for the actions of government. Others may have assumed that anything which is legal is also moral, therefore there is no moral law applicable to the actions of men committed in the name of government. Still others may assume that, although there may be a moral law making men accountable for government action, no one knows what that law is, and it is therefore impossible to distinguish between good and bad in government.

Let us discuss under the following headings the possibility that we are exercising unrighteous dominion upon each other by abusing the police power:

(1) Is the individual morally responsible for government action?

(2) Can government exercise unrighteous dominion on behalf of the individual?

(3) How may one determine if his government is exercising unrighteous dominion?

IS THE INDIVIDUAL MORALLY RESPONSIBLE FOR GOVERNMENT ACTION?

Under a dictatorship or monarchy where the private citizen has no voice in the conduct of government, it would obviously be unjust to hold him accountable for compulsion used by it. In a republic where government action is subject to control by the voting citizen, there is no other place to rest the credit or blame. If the citizen is not accountable, then who is? We are the ones who pass judgment upon candidates, platforms, and issues. The power to elect or defeat rests entirely in our hands.

The scriptures state plainly that the Lord holds the individual responsible under the republic which He caused to be established in this land:

> We believe that governments were instituted of God for the benefit of man; and that he holds men accountable for their acts, in relation to them, both in making laws and administering them for the good and safety of society. (D&C 134:1)

When the individual disapproves of an unjust government measure and uses all of his influence against it, no blame should be attached. Justice demands that each be held liable only for those acts which have his approval and support. Since laws may be good as well as evil, opposition to a good law may be as blameworthy as approval of a bad one. Where one does sanction the use of force, it would appear he is just as answerable as if he had exercised it himself.

This position may seem novel to those who regard government as if it had an existence independent of human beings—an undefinable, phantom entity possessing the power to pursue objectives of its own. Such a view is unrealistic and one who takes it is deceiving himself. The actions of government are the actions of men—performed by men at the command of men—and someone is going to be held morally accountable for every act performed in the name of government. In a republic such as ours, the someone is everyone—everyone who sanctions the act.

What an awesome responsibility we take upon ourselves when we support the adoption of a law! Men speak constantly of the privilege of living under a republican form of government. Perhaps we should spend more time considering the enormous power we wield and the terrible penalties we may suffer if we abuse that power.

Some of us may go through life hardly realizing that compulsion and the threat of compulsion are used to secure compliance with every law enacted. We, the individuals who support such laws, have utilized this compulsion to prohibit every human act which would have been performed except for the adoption of such law. Also we have compelled the performance of every human act which would not have been performed except therefor.

CAN GOVERNMENT EXERCISE UNRIGHTEOUS DOMINION ON BEHALF OF THE INDIVIDUAL?

Any act of compulsion which one can perform alone, he can commit in concert with others. The greater the number who combine their efforts, the more certain is their success. When coercion is imposed in the name of government, success is almost guaranteed since those doing the compelling are using the supreme physical force in society. This force is being supplied by the mass of the people with arms and men for the specific purpose of using compulsion.

Governments deal in nothing but force and the threat thereof. This is the exclusive means by which they act. They exist for the sole purpose of adopting and enforcing rules governing human conduct. These rules or laws are enforced in one of three ways—by taking from the disobedient either his life, his liberty, or his property. Every law has attached to it a penalty for disobedience which prescribes one or more of these three forms of physical punishment. This is the very essence of compulsion.

In a nation of law-abiding citizens it is easy to forget that the only reason for adopting a law is to compel those to obey it who would not do so unless threatened with a loss of their life, liberty, or property. When the laws are seldom disobeyed, we rarely have the opportunity to observe the use of physical coercion. But, the police power is always there ready to act if someone defies the decrees of the state. It is the threat of the use of force which does the compelling in most cases, and people generally obey without the necessity of being handled by the police.

The pages of history are replete with instances of governments being used to destroy individual freedom. When used for this purpose they are horribly efficient. Without question, the number of crimes committed by men in the name of government exceed by many times those committed by men acting individually. The wanton destruction of life, liberty, and property which occurs when an aggressor nation makes war is incalculable. When we also consider those millions of citizens who have been murdered, enslaved, and plundered by their own governments, it becomes clear beyond doubt that the greatest threat to freedom on earth is man acting through the agency of his government.

HOW MAY ONE DETERMINE IF HIS GOVERNMENT IS EXERCISING UNRIGHTEOUS DOMINION?

If the Lord is going to hold each of us morally accountable for every coercive act of government of which we approve, it is of the utmost importance that we be able to accurately discern the good from the evil in government action. It is not enough that we do this approximately. We must be able to distinguish with precision because:

> When we undertake to...exercise control or dominion or compulsion...*in any degree of unrighteousness*...Amen to the priesthood or the authority of that man. (D&C 121:37 {author's emphasis})

Is not the Lord expecting too much in requiring the ordinary citizen to know with certainty that line which divides right from wrong in government action? Is it reasonable to believe that He would deprive a man of his Priesthood because he had failed to detect even the slightest degree of unrighteous dominion in every law which came to his attention, no matter what his training, background, or experience?

Those accustomed to relying on the learning of men and the wisdom of the world to teach them the art of government may consider it absurd to expect so much of the voting public. They may believe the common man largely unequipped to make such fine distinctions. How does the Lord view the matter? Does He believe men are sufficiently instructed to pass judgment upon their own laws?

We are told in D&C 134:1 that He holds us accountable for our acts in relation to government, both in making laws and administering them. How can He do this? Very simply, He merely requires each of us to apply exactly that same test of right and wrong to the actions of government as we do to every other act for which we are responsible; this is the test of conscience.

If those who adopt and execute laws are our agents, doing our bidding, we should never ask them to do anything we would consider evil or wrong for us to do ourselves. Every person who knows right from wrong can apply this test as quickly and as easily in the case of government as in any other moral decision. We need only realize that an act performed by public servants which has our approval makes us equally as responsible as if we had done it ourselves. We should apply the same test of conscience.

Who will contend that the Lord uses one moral law when the individual acts alone and still a different one when he acts jointly with others whether in a gang, a mob, or a government? The thought is contrary to reason as well as the scriptures which explicitly tell us we should never use the police power in such a way as to violate conscience:

> The civil magistrate should restrain crime, but never control conscience; should punish guilt, but never suppress the freedom of the soul...all governments have a right to enact such laws as in their own judgments are best calculated to secure the public interest; at the same time, however, holding sacred the freedom of conscience. (D&C 134:4, 5)

34

This same prohibition against using the police power in such a way as to violate the conscience or belief of the individual was imposed upon the Nephites when the Lord caused a government by the voice of the people to be established among them:

> For there was a law that men should be judged according to their crimes. Nevertheless, there was no law against a man's belief; therefore, a man was punished only for the crimes which he had done; therefore all men were on equal grounds. (Alma 30:11)

Since the only conscience we really know is our own, it is the only one we can use or violate. In determining those circumstances under which we would consider it proper to deprive our fellowman of his life, liberty, or property, it is necessary that we mentally place ourselves in his position before we accurately know what our conscience tells us. We must apply Christ's *Golden Rule* which says:

> Therefore, all things whatsoever ye would that men should do to you, do ye even so to them: for this is the law and the prophets. (Matt. 7:12; 3 Ne. 14:12)

Each normal person senses immediately an injustice done to him. His reason tells him that others will react the same way. The scriptures also tell us that all men may know right from wrong:

> For behold, the Spirit of Christ is given to every man, that he may know good from evil. (Moroni 7:16 See also D&C 84:46.)

Every person is capable of answering this all-important problem of government: Under what circumstances is it proper to use coercion?

The answer demanded by both logic and our moral sense of right and wrong is: Only when we would consider it just to have the same force used against ourselves. Thus, in passing judgment upon our neighbor's actions, we pass judgment upon our own. If we feel we should be free to do as we please under a given set of conditions without fear of punishment, the Golden Rule demands we allow our fellow men the same latitude.

In the Golden Rule we have found Christ's answer to the following question discussed above:

> Under what circumstances does a group of men have the moral right to forcibly deprive their fellow man of his life, liberty, or property?

The Golden Rule provides a reliable and very simple standard by which we may each determine for ourselves what actions of government are good and what are bad. Not only is it a test, but it is the only test based upon moral law which exists. If we do not use the Golden Rule and the test of conscience, we are without any standard at all which is based upon considerations of good and evil. The individual conscience is the only place we can go to distinguish between right and wrong.

It will be recalled that in discussing the law of retribution it was concluded that the only justification for forcibly depriving another of one of the elements of freedom was for the purpose of enforcing this law. In other words, if one commits an evil act by destroying an element of his neighbor's freedom, it is proper to punish him by depriving him of some element of his own freedom. Let us demonstrate that this is the same test we use when we apply the Golden Rule.

No person would consider it just to be punished for anything except an evil act. The Golden Rule insists that we use force upon our neighbor only for this same purpose. Under the law of retribution, we justify the use of force only for the purpose of punishing one who, without justification, destroyed freedom. The destruction of freedom is equivalent to committing evil; therefore the rules are identical.

Let us apply these underlying moral imperatives to specific acts of government, and in doing so, present scriptural support for our conclusions. We shall first examine those cases in which the Lord has given His approval for using the force of government against the individual. Then we shall note some of those acts which are a violation of conscience and, consequently, an exercise of unrighteous dominion.

36

CHAPTER VI

THOSE CIRCUMSTANCES UNDER WHICH GOD HAS AUTHORIZED USE OF THE FORCE OF GOVERNMENT AGAINST THE INDIVIDUAL

The Lord justifies the use of the police power against the individual for the purpose of executing the divine law of retribution. The specific circumstances under which He has given His approval for this use of force may be classified under the following four headings:

(1) To punish criminals,
(2) To wage defensive war and provide for the nation's defense,
(3) To enforce the right and control of private property,
(4) To compel the citizen to bear his fair share of the burden of supporting the government in performing the above three functions.

Let us discuss each of these four cases.

PUNISHMENT OF CRIMINALS

In numerous places in the scriptures the Lord justifies the use of the police power to punish criminals. He prescribes the death penalty in the case of murder. He tells us that our failure to execute this divine command will condemn us. When Nehor, who slew Gideon, was brought to be judged of his crime, Alma, the Chief Judge, spoke to him as follows:

> And thou hast shed the blood of a righteous man, yea, a man who had done much good among this people; and were we to spare thee his blood would come upon us for vengeance. (Alma 1:13)

The death penalty for murder is mentioned several times in the Nephite scriptures and is indicated in D&C 42:19. Doctrine and Covenants, Section 134 consists of *A Declaration of Belief Regarding Governments and Laws in General.* Included therein is a statement of our belief concerning the punishment of crimes generally, which reads as follows:

> We believe that the commission of crime should be punished according to the nature of the offense; that murder, treason, robbery, theft, and the breach of the general peace, in all respects, should be punished according to their criminality and their tendency to evil among men, by the laws of that government in which the offense is committed;...(D&C 134:8)

This statement is one with which men in general will agree because it conforms to our sense of justice. While man may disagree about what constitutes proper punishment for a given crime, throughout the ages they have uniformly inflicted some form of punishment upon criminals. It is clear that the use of the police power to punish crime satisfies the test of conscience as contained in the laws of God. It has been shown heretofore that this is a vital part of enforcing the law of retribution.

WAGE DEFENSIVE WAR

Doctrine and Covenants, Section 98 contains a statement of those circumstances under which a nation is justified in going out to battle.

...if he has sought thy life, and thy life is endangered by him, thine enemy is in thine hands and thou art justified.

Behold, this is the law I gave unto my servant Nephi, and thy fathers, Joseph, and Jacob, and Isaac, and Abraham, and all mine ancient prophets and apostles. (D&C 98:31-32)

War is authorized only as a defensive measure after the aggressor nation has refused to heed a plea for peace. This is the same law which the Lord gave to the Nephites:

And they (the Nephites) were doing that which they felt was the duty which they owed to their God; for the Lord had said unto them, and also unto their fathers, that: Inasmuch as ye are not guilty of the first offense, neither the second, ye shall not suffer yourselves to be slain by the hands of your enemies. And again, the Lord has said that: Ye shall defend your families even unto bloodshed...(Alma 43:46-47).

A further clarification of the Lord's commandments to them regarding war is found in the following passage:

Now the Nephites were taught to defend themselves against their enemies, even to the shedding of blood if it were necessary; yea; and they were also taught never to give an offense, yea, and never to raise the sword except it were to preserve their lives. (Alma 48:14)

Since aggressive warfare is a form of criminal activity, the same considerations of conscience which justify the use of force to punish internal crime and satisfy the law of retribution are equally applicable here.

ENFORCEMENT OF THE RIGHT AND CONTROL OF PRIVATE PROPERTY

Doctrine and Covenants 134:2 reads as follows:

We believe that no government can exist in peace, except such laws are framed and held inviolate as will secure to each individual the free exercise of conscience, the right and control of property, and the protection of life.

Protection of the right and control of property is one of the main reasons for the existence of government. The above scripture indicates that peace is impossible unless this basic human right is recognized and enforced.

The Nephites used the police power to protect this right as is shown by the following quotation:

> Now if a man owed another, and he would not pay that which he did owe, he was complained of to the judge; and the judge executed authority, and sent forth officers that the man should be brought before him; and he judged the man according to the law and the evidences which were brought against him and thus the man was compelled to pay that which he owed, or be stripped, or be cast out from among the people as a thief and a robber. (Alma 11:2)

Property is derived from labor. Moral man has always recognized that the wealth produced by a person belonged to him. Theft, robbery, arson and all other forms of taking or destroying another's property have always been regarded as both evil and criminal. The use of the police power to compel a person to pay an honest debt or to surrender to its rightful owner property which he unlawfully holds, is strictly in accord with the dictates of conscience.

As will be pointed out hereafter more fully, the same moral considerations which preclude a person or a group of persons from using force to unjustly deprive another of his property, apply equally when they use the force of government for the same immoral purposes.

COMPEL THE CITIZEN TO SUPPORT HIS GOVERNMENT

Governments exist for the purpose of protecting the lives, liberties, and properties of their citizens. It is only right that those who receive these benefits should bear their fair share of the cost of such protection. As is stated in D&C 134:5:

> We believe that all men are bound to sustain and uphold the respective governments in which they reside, while protected in their inherent and inalienable rights by the laws of such governments.

The Book of Mormon provides an interesting case history wherein the Lord justified the use of force to compel the citizens to provide men and materials necessary to the defense of the nation. Moroni, the supreme commander of the Nephites, was waging a two-front war against numerically superior foes who had invaded Nephite lands. The failure of the home-front to support the armies in the field created a crisis which caused this great patriot to threaten the leaders of his own government with reprisals if they did not come to his aid.

His epistle to the head of government, ordering him to furnish men and supplies under the threat of death if he did not, has been copied into the record by Mormon, the historian. Excerpts from this epistle follow:

> And now, except ye do repent of that which ye have done, and begin to be up and doing, and send forth food and men unto us, and also unto Helaman, that he may support those parts of our country which he has regained, and that we may also recover the remainder of our possessions in these parts, behold it will be expedient that we contend no more with the Lamanites until we have first cleansed our inward vessel, yea, even the great head of our government....Behold, the Lord saith unto me: If those whom ye have appointed your governors do not repent of their sins and iniquities, ye shall go up to battle against them. (Alma 60:24, 33)

The use of the police power to compel the citizen to pay his taxes, serve in the armed forces, and otherwise support his government in protecting him, makes possible its existence in the first place. Indeed the protection of life, liberty and property in our society would be rendered virtually impossible without it. There is no violation of conscience in requiring those who are protected to pay their fair share of the cost of what they need and receive.

41

On the contrary, each citizen who lives under a government which protects his freedom should consider it not only a duty but a privilege to give of his time and means for its support. Seldom in the history of nations has the common man been permitted to participate in the governing process. The right and duty of self-government provides a rare opportunity to labor for the cause of freedom, to learn firsthand the operation of the law of retribution and to cooperate with the Lord in enforcing it.

The great danger, however, of being given this power is that we will abuse it because,

> We have learned by sad experience that it is the nature and disposition of almost all men, as soon as they get a little authority, as they suppose, they will immediately begin to exercise unrighteous dominion. (D&C 121:39)

Let us examine the possibility that we citizens of the United States are exercising unrighteous dominion upon one another by directing the police power to do things which go beyond enforcing the law of retribution and therefore offend the conscience and violate the Golden Rule.

HAROLD B. LEE

There are some things of which I am sure, and that is that contrary to the belief and mistaken ideas of some people, the United Order will not be a socialistic or communistic setup... (Harold B. Lee, *Stand Ye in Holy Places,* p. 280)

Now, keep in mind with all the crowding in of the socialistic reform programs that are threatening the very foundation of the Church, we must never forget what the Lord said, "that the church may stand independent above all other creatures beneath the celestial world" (D&C 78:14). Whenever we allow ourselves to become entangled and have to be subsidized from government sources—and we think that it's the expedient way to do business in this day—or when we yield to such pressures, I warn you that government subsidies are not the Lord's way; and if we begin to accept, we are on our way to becoming subsidized politically as well as financially. (Harold B. Lee, *The Teachings of Harold B. Lee,* [1996], p. 314-115)

CHAPTER VII

ACTS OF GOVERNMENT WHICH CONSTITUTE AN EXERCISE OF UNRIGHTEOUS DOMINION

Men may exercise unrighteous dominion upon one another through the agency of government in just as many ways as they can when acting outside its framework. The most common method, however, is by denying or interfering with the right to own and control property, one of the elements of freedom. The following welfare state practices typify the methods used.

PLUNDER BY GOVERNMENT

Government can give nothing to one person unless it has first taken something from someone else. This taking is usually in the form of taxes which the taxpayer is compelled to pay at the risk of having his property taken by force. How would you regard compulsory taking if performed without being legalized?

Suppose it were suggested that you join a group that was going to use force to take part of the property from a wealthy citizen "A" and give it to "B" who had but little, or divide it among your group who were also "poor." Would it violate your conscience to do this?

Or, applying the Golden Rule, put yourself in "A's" shoes. He has already given all he desires to charity. Are you not violating his conscience when you compel him to give more? Would you enjoy having someone dictate how much you must give to your church, a hospital or a college? Would not this be a plain case of theft? And if you pass a law and legalize the taking and the giving, have you really changed the essential nature of the act? Haven't you merely legalized stealing?

Another problem which should worry those favoring plunder by government is this: How much of "A's" property should be taken—10%, 20%, or more? What answer are you going to give to the socialists and communists who propose taking 100% and then returning to "A" only what he "needs"? Is there any valid moral distinction between taking one half or all? Is it not an exercise of unrighteous dominion to forcibly take any property from one to whom it belongs and give it to another to whom it does not belong? Each person must let his own conscience determine this, with the risk that if he reaches the wrong conclusion, *Amen to the priesthood or the authority of that man.*

President David O. Mckay has given his views on the matter in these words:

> We are placed on this earth to work, to live; and the earth will give us a living. It is our duty to strive to make a success of what we possess—to till the earth, subdue matter, conquer the glebe, take care of the cattle, the flocks and the herds. It is the Government's duty to see that you are protected in these efforts, and no other man has the right to deprive you of any of your privileges. But it is not the Government's duty to support you. That is one reason why I shall raise my voice as long as God gives me sound or ability, against this Communistic idea that the Government will take care of us all, and everything belongs to the Government. It is wrong! No wonder, in trying to perpetuate that idea, they become anti-Christ, because that doctrine strikes directly against the doctrine of the Saviour.... No government owes you a living. You get it yourself by your own acts!—never by trespassing upon the rights of a neighbor; *never by cheating him.* You put a blemish upon your character the moment you do. ({Author's emphasis} *Statements on Communism and the Constitution of the United States.* p. 23, Deseret Book Co., 1966)

45

There are those who will insist that some people absolutely must receive assistance and that we simply cannot allow them to starve. It is hoped that everyone will agree to this and when we observe anyone suffering from want, we will administer to their needs.

Stating the matter in this form does not recognize the extremely important moral problem of "taking" which is unavoidably a part of government charity. Let us restate the proposition so as to include the entire moral question. If you saw one person in need and another with plenty, would you use force to compel a more equal division? Would it violate your conscience to physically coerce one neighbor to share his means with another?

Most people agree that each person has a moral obligation to be charitable, but is it morally right for us to compel others to be as charitable as we think they should be? Is it not rather our moral obligation to allow them to determine for themselves how much they shall give?

If those who are wealthy fail to voluntarily impart of their substance to the poor, they will be adequately punished by the Lord for their selfishness. (D&C 104:18) If, through the force of government or otherwise they are compelled to divide with those in need, how can the Lord either bless them for being charitable or punish them for being uncharitable? The same freedom which permits men to do evil permits them to do good. If you destroy one, you have destroyed both and made freedom of choice, with its consequent rewards and punishments, impossible.

When those who are poor undertake to obtain their sustenance without working for it, they bring themselves under condemnation. The Lord has indicated in the following sequence of verses that the poor whose hands are not stayed from laying hold upon other men's goods will suffer punishment along with the selfish rich:

> Wo unto you rich men, that will not give your substance to the poor, for your riches will canker your souls; and this shall be your lamentation in the day of visitation, and of judgment, and of indignation: the harvest is past, the summer is ended, and my soul is not saved!
>
> Wo unto you poor men, whose hearts are not broken, whose spirits are not contrite, and whose bellies are not satisfied, and whose hands are not stayed from laying hold

upon other men's goods, whose eyes are full of greediness, and who will not labor with your own hands!" (D&C 56:16-17)

GOVERNMENT ENFORCED MONOPOLIES

Another questionable but extremely common practice is to use the police power to give ourselves monopolistic protection against competitors. This would be called a criminal conspiracy and branded as extortion if forcibly engaged in without government protection and approval.

Today in the United States, monopoly protection is afforded by the police power in nearly every line of economic activity: in the professions and trades; in transportation and communication; in agriculture and labor; in finance, banking, and many other lines. □ How does this vast system of government enforced monopolies stand the conscience test and the application of the Golden Rule?

If we desire for ourselves the freedom to enter a trade or occupation when and where we choose, we should allow our fellow men this same right. If we believe we should be left free to purchase goods or services from any person who offers them for sale, how can we forcibly restrict the freedom of other members of the buying public and still live the Golden Rule?

President McKay has counseled us against prohibiting others from pursuing the occupation of their choice. He said:

> It is a great imposition, if indeed not a crime, for any government, any labor union, or any other organization to deny a man the right to speak, to worship, and to work. *(Statements on Communism and the Constitution of the United States.* p. 17. Deseret Book Co. 1966)

The prophet, Joseph Smith, expressed a similar view to the council of the City of Nauvoo:

> I also spoke at length for the repeal of the ordinance of the city licensing merchants, hawkers, taverns, and ordinaries, desiring that this might be a free people, and enjoy equal

rights and privileges, and the ordinances were repealed. (*History of the Church,* Vol. 6, p. 8)

And finally the Lord has warned us against the use of extortion in acquiring the goods of this world:

> Yea, all things which come of the earth, in the season thereof, are made for the benefit and the use of man, both to please the eye and to gladden the heart;
> And it pleaseth God that he hath given all these things unto man; for unto this end were they made to be used, with judgment, not to excess, neither by extortion. (D&C 59:18, 20)

Men use a variety of arguments to justify the use of the police power to restrict competition. Some claim there is over-production of the commodities or services they are offering. When one considers the millions who are classified as paupers in every nation on earth with death and want in many places, how can it be asserted that there is an oversupply of any form of organized wealth? True, there are raw materials, and energy in abundance but man's desire for the finished product is insatiable and always exceeds the supply.

Still others argue that open competition in their field should be prohibited because, if this were not done, the unlearned, the unskilled, and the inexperienced would be serving the public. But this argument assumes it is possible to classify men into two groups—the qualified and the unqualified. Is this assumption valid?

Let us investigate this matter by first observing that no one is perfect. There never was and there never will be a professional or business man who could not benefit from more knowledge, training, experience, skill, and better facilities with which to serve the public. This fact must be faced: there are not two groups of men—the qualified and the unqualified; there is only one group and every member of it is unqualified to some extent.

This being true, the only choice open is between varying degrees of incompetence, inexperience, and ignorance. Now is there a man living who can honestly claim that he is able to make a division of this group, confer special privileges on one segment which are denied to the other, and still be fair to everyone? What rational basis exists for determining where the line should be drawn? How much training or experience should be required before permitting a person to offer his services to the public—6 weeks, 6 months, 6 years, or double one of these periods? It is impossible for men to reach agreement on this problem or for any person to say with certainty he is right in his opinion and all who disagree are wrong.

It is also impossible to reach agreement on who should be given the power to set up the qualifications for engaging in a given economic activity and force their views on all others. Some may contend that those already engaged in the profession, trade, or business should have this privilege. Others would confer the power upon some agency of government. Still others contend that the matter should be settled by majority vote.

Since all men are to a greater or lesser extent unqualified to serve the public, and since it is impossible to find a fair or a logical basis for making a division of the unqualified, and since it is also impossible to reach agreement on who should be given the power to confer special privileges on some which are denied to others, why not leave the decision to the only person who has a moral right to make it—the one who is paying the bill? Why not adopt a policy which allows every member of the consuming public to decide for himself how much education, experience, facilities, etc. are necessary to engage in a profession or a business? No one can devise a more equitable method than this.

If those who hold themselves out to serve the public misrepresent the extent of their training and experience or otherwise act in a criminal manner, they should be punished for such wrongdoing by the police power. One form of punishment might be to deny them the privilege of engaging in such activities for a specified period of time. Also, if they perform their work negligently and cause injury, they may be held liable to those who have suffered damage.

But why should we prejudge them? Why should we impose prior restraints and threaten them with jail or fine for even attempting to serve the public in their chosen field? They may do much good and no harm. Their services may be needed.

If those who consider themselves better trained than others desire to form an exclusive professional group and limit membership to applicants who have met certain minimum requirements, this should be their privilege and no one should interfere with it.

Furthermore, if they desire to inform the public as to whom they consider qualified to engage in a given profession, trade, or business, this basic right should be protected.

But to give one partially qualified group (or their government agents) the power to forcibly prevent those they consider less qualified from competing is rank discrimination and an abuse of the power of government.

D&C 134:5 tells us very plainly that, *the civil magistrate should restrain crime, but never suppress the freedom of the soul.* It is a direct violation of this scripture for us to direct our agents in government to punish our fellow men for engaging in perfectly legitimate business or professional activities. We do not *restrain crime* or *punish guilt* when we do this, but we do *suppress the freedom of the soul.*

When we use the police power to prevent our fellow men from buying goods and services from whomsoever they desire we are treating them as children or mental incompetents who are unable to make their own decisions. We are either prohibiting them from purchasing a desired commodity or service or compelling them to trade with someone they would not have patronized had we allowed them their freedom in the matter.

When we direct our bureaucratic servants to forcibly prevent a farmer from raising certain crops on his own land; when we deny the youth who emerge from our schools the right to work at any trade, business, or profession they desire without first getting the exact amount of training we have decreed and obtaining the express consent of our government agents; when we substitute our own judgment for that of our fellow men and threaten them with a loss of their life, liberty, or property if they engage in perfectly legitimate economic pursuits except in accordance with rules we have laid down, we have clearly done things which we would consider highly immoral if done outside the framework of government.

How can we bring ourselves to do these things to one another? Are we deceiving ourselves as to the real reason behind our actions? Could it be that instead of fearing overproduction of the goods or services we offer for sale, we really are trying to create a scarcity so that we can enrich ourselves with the higher prices restrictive legislation permits us to charge?

Is it possible that, instead of fearing that some untrained novice will injure society by offering inferior services, we are really using the force of law to create an exclusive class of citizens to which only a select few may belong? With these questions in mind let us consider the following scripture:

> Behold, there are many called, but few are chosen. And why are they not chosen? Because their hearts are set so much upon the things of this world, and aspire to the honors of men, that they do not learn this one lesson...that the powers of heaven cannot be controlled nor handled only upon the principles of righteousness. (D&C 121:34-36)

We might also ask ourselves if, when we forcibly prevent the buying public from patronizing anyone they desire, we are not proving the accuracy of the following judgment and penalty pronounced by the Lord upon men in general:

> We have learned by sad experience that it is the nature and disposition of almost all men, as soon as they get a little authority, as they suppose, they will immediately begin to exercise unrighteous dominion.
> Hence, many are called, but few are chosen. (D&C 121:39-40)

REGIMENTATION

There is an enormous amount of regulation and regimentation of the private and business affairs of the people carried on by government at our express command and with our approval. Let us examine our consciences about the morality of what we are doing to each other.

We might start by asking by what right do I tell an employer whom he can hire, what wages he can pay, or how many hours he can work his employees? Or looking at it from the employee's position: Where did I get the authority to forcibly prevent him from working as many hours as he desires at any wage he considers appropriate? Can I visualize myself meddling in these people's affairs and dictating their contract terms outside the framework of government? Passing a law changes neither the officious nature of my conduct nor my moral responsibility therefor.

It violates every rule of good taste and common sense for me to force my views upon my neighbors in this manner. How then do I justify my sending the police and the bureaucrats out to regiment them on my behalf? Am I not violating my conscience as well as the Golden Rule? Putting myself in their place, would I desire to be dictated to in these matters, or would I want the freedom to make my own decisions?

What does my conscience tell me about compelling people to save for their old age under the social security laws, whether they want to or not? What justification do I find for entering the innermost affairs of their lives, and forcing them to buy medical, industrial, unemployment, and liability insurance? Such questions might be continued for pages, because government regulation-both state and federal-has now reached nearly every aspect of our private lives.

The people of the United States who are slavishly complying with these multitudinous rules and regulations are doing so under the threat of being punished with a forcible deprivation of our lives, liberties and properties if we don't comply. And who is threatening us? We are doing it to one another. One wonders if we are not living in those days foreseen by the prophet Isaiah when he said:

> And the people shall be oppressed, every one by another, and every one by his neighbor; the child shall behave himself proudly against the ancient, and the base against the honorable. (Isaiah 3:5; 2 Nephi 13:5)

When we engage in the practice of regimenting the lives of our neighbors, not only are we exercising unrighteous dominion but we are jeopardizing the continued existence of our constitutional form of government. President McKay has said:

> Unwise legislation, too often prompted by political expediency is periodically being enacted that seductively undermines man's right of free agency, robs him of his rightful liberties, and makes him but a cog in the crushing wheel of regimentation which, if persisted in, will end in dictatorship. (*Statements on Communism and the Constitution of the United States*. p. 10, Deseret Book Co. 1966)

52

Each person who believes in the Golden Rule and the divine law of retribution might do well to re-examine his own views on government and ask—Am I using it only for the purpose of punishing evil as the Lord has directed, or am I one of those 'social engineers' who believes the common man is too selfish and foolish to be left free to spend his own money, make his own contracts, run his own business, and provide for his own future?

When men resort to the use of the force of government to solve all social problems, they demonstrate a loss of faith in God. In place of that faith they have substituted reliance on the *arm of flesh*.

The more completely one believes in the omnipotence, omniscience, and justice of God, the more willing he is to accept Christ's philosophy of freedom. Such a believer knows-nothing doubting, that no matter what he, or any other man does, every person will receive exactly what he deserves.

On the other hand, those who deny the existence of God tend to judge everything from a materialistic viewpoint. Their idea of justice consists of an equal distribution of the material comforts and bodily needs of the world—food, clothing, shelter, medicine, education, etc. They assume that since there is no divine law of justice in operation, they must use force to bring about equality. They would use government for this purpose.

If one looks about him in the world, he will discover numerous illustrations of this relationship between faith in God and belief in freedom on the one hand, atheism and belief in slavery on the other. It is no accident that those who established our constitutional government of freedom adopted as their motto, IN GOD WE TRUST, while those who founded the Communist tyranny were avowed atheists committed to the destruction of religion and freedom.

One who accepts the plain words of the scriptures knows that it is impossible for any one to defeat God's justice. The Lord is not relying upon man or the puny efforts of his government to banish poverty, alleviate pain, and administer to the ills of society by using compulsion. Justice will be done in spite of anything we do or fail to do.

Some may conclude that if everyone is going to receive exactly what he deserves regardless of anything I do or my government does or fails to do, there is no point in doing anything at all. One who takes such an attitude leaves out of consideration the most important element of all—the eternal welfare of his own soul.

No one of us is capable of determining the destiny of anyone else. God has placed it within our power to determine our own with His help. He has so arranged things that each person is provided with those opportunities and capabilities to which his past conduct has entitled him and we should never forget that the Lord is the source of all blessings. His plan of justice allows each one the exclusive right to determine those blessings or punishments he will receive.

Our reward is largely determined by the attitude we take toward the problems of others. If we sincerely believe in charity and give of ourselves and our means to feed the hungry, clothe the naked, and visit the widows and the fatherless, Christ has promised us a place in His kingdom on His right hand. (Matt. 25:31-46)

If we try to solve the problems of poverty, ignorance, and suffering by forcing others to be charitable and by denying people the freedom to make their own mistakes, we have adopted Satan's plan and have subjected ourselves to him to the same extent. Even a partial adoption of his methods will condemn us because when we undertake to exercise dominion in any degree of unrighteousness, *Amen to the priesthood or the authority of that man.*

CHAPTER VIII

ANOTHER STANDARD BY WHICH TO JUDGE GOVERNMENT ACTION — THE UNITED STATES CONSTITUTION AND THE COMMUNIST MANIFESTO

In a speech delivered at Brigham Young University in Provo, Utah, on May 18, 1960, President David O. McKay said:

> I come with another theme this morning—Two Contending Forces. Those forces are known and have been designated by different terms throughout the ages. 'In the Beginning' they were known as Satan on the one hand, and Christ on the other...In these days they are called...Communism on the one hand, free agency on the other.

Thus has the prophet of God in our day, identified the form of government proposed by Satan for our acceptance. Just as the government authorized by the Lord has a Constitution, so does this one authored by Satan—it is the Communist Manifesto drafted by Karl Marx in 1848. It is generally regarded as the ultimate in authority for Communists the world over. On the other hand the Lord has placed His stamp of approval on the United States Constitution. (D&C 98:4-7)

Having these two documents—the United States Constitution and the Communist Manifesto-available for comparison, simplifies the problem of distinguishing right from wrong in government. The two systems proposed by these documents are the very antithesis of each other. They contradict and oppose each other at every point.

While the Constitution provides for a federal system with the powers of government first divided between the state and the national, and with a second division between the legislative, executive and judicial, the Communist form is a single, centralized, all-powerful dictatorship. The Constitution contains a Bill of Rights and other detailed limitations upon the power of government over the☐ individual. The Communist state has no restraints whatsoever. While the Constitution guarantees citizens the right to elect their own political leaders and to make alterations in their laws, Communism denies all rights of self-government.

There is one basic objective to which Communism is committed which stamps it as the mortal enemy of the Lord's form of government: this is it's unalterable opposition to the right of private property. The Constitution expressly guarantees the protection of this right in the same clause in which it protects the rights of life and liberty, and it denies government the power to take from the individual his private property for public use without just compensation.

On the other hand the Manifesto declares that the destruction of private property is the primary and basic aim of Communism. It says:

> In this sense the theory of the Communists may be summed up in the single sentence: abolition of private property.

At still another place in the Manifesto we find this:

> The Communist revolution is the most radical rupture with traditional property relations.

Not only does the Manifesto declare its main purpose to be the destruction of private property, but it contains a detailed plan by which this is to be accomplished in a nation such as the United States whose laws and constitutions were designed to protect this right.

The method proposed is not violent and bloody revolution (at least at the outset) but the peaceful and legal process of inducing the citizens of the United States and other nations to destroy the right themselves with their own legislatures, courts, and executives. We are to adopt a series of laws which will inevitably have this result. Listen to the Manifesto as it unfolds its plan:

> We have seen above that the first step in the revolution by the working class is to raise the proletariat to the position of ruling class, to establish democracy. The proletariat will use its political supremacy to wrest by degrees all capital from the bourgeoisie (property owners), to centralize all instruments of production in the hands of the state.

This naked appeal to the selfishness of the voter to use the government as an instrument of plunder is nothing but a proposal for legalized theft. The Manifesto goes on to say:

> Of course in the beginning this cannot be effected except by means of despotic inroads on the rights of property and on the conditions of bourgeois production:...These measures will, of course, be different in different countries. Nevertheless, in the most advanced countries the following will be pretty generally applicable...

Then follows the famous ten points of the Communist Manifesto. They constitute a blueprint for legislative action. They are in essence a political platform to be adopted over a period of time which culminates in the complete destruction of private property.

There are a variety of ways in which a government can destroy private property and the Manifesto's ten points include most of them. One way, of course, is to confiscate by outright seizure. This method is proposed in points numbered one and four which read:

1. Abolition of property in land and application of all rents of land to public purposes.
4. Confiscation of the property of all emigrants and rebels.

To what extent have we adopted the policy of government ownership of land in the United States? The Federal Government has always owned land, but up until recently its policy was to transfer its holdings to private owners either under homestead laws or by grants of various kinds. This policy no longer prevails, and today it is reported that the Federal Government is condemning for "public purposes" thousands of acres of land each year for such things as power projects, housing projects, irrigation schemes and flood control. The Federal Government owns approximately one-fourth of all land in the continental United States today.

The second method for destroying private property proposed by the Manifesto is this:

2. A heavy progressive or graduated income tax.

The founding fathers of our nation, well aware that *the power to tax is the power to destroy,* included within the Constitution severe restrictions upon the power of the Federal Government to impose direct taxes. Such were forbidden unless proportioned according to census. When this nation adopted the 16th amendment to the Constitution in 1913, it abandoned this safeguard to human rights provided by the Lord's form of government and substituted therefor Satan's proposal for their destruction.

The power of government to impose graduated taxes when coupled with the power to produce inflation with "printing press money," is an extremely potent combination for destroying property. By the simple device of cranking the printing presses, thereby raising prices and wages, the government can silently elevate everyone into a higher tax bracket without changing the tax rate structure at all.

The public is deceived into believing that their higher wages and incomes brought about by inflation are beneficial. In actuality their purchasing power is not increased by the raise but rather is decreased because of the heavier tax rates they are subject to and the higher prices they pay for what they purchase.

3. Abolition of all right of inheritance.

The 16th Amendment which permitted the imposition of graduated income taxes also allowed steeply graduated inheritance and gift taxes. The federal estate tax rate rises to 77% and goes a long way toward achieving the *abolition of all right of inheritance* proposed by the Manifesto. And here again, if inflation continues at its present rate, everyone will soon find himself in these upper tax brackets and the right of a person to leave his property to those he loves either during life or at death will have been destroyed. Thus another stated objective of the Communists will have been reached.

5. Centralization of credit in the hands of the state by means of a national bank with state capital and an exclusive monopoly.

Even John Maynard Keynes, one of the most vigorous proponents of the welfare state, recognized in this Communist device a potent weapon for the destruction and confiscation of private property by the state. Said he:

> Lenin (first Communist dictator in Russia) is said to have declared that the best way to destroy the Capitalist System was to debauch the currency. By a continuing process of inflation, governments can confiscate, secretly and unobserved, an important part of the wealth of their citizens...Lenin was certainly right. There is no subtler, no surer means of over-turning the existing basis of society than to debauch the currency. The process engages all the hidden forces of economic law on the side of destruction, and does it in a manner which not one man in a million is able to diagnose. (*Economic Consequences of the Peace, Keynes.* Harcourt, Brace and Howe, 1920, pp. 235-236)

The Constitutional Convention specifically rejected a proposal to give the Federal government the power to issue "paper money." (*Elliot's Debates,* Vol. V, pp. 434-435) The men who attended that Convention were painfully aware of the great dangers of paper money. Governments with the power to print paper money have always abused this power. Many of the Convention attendees had participated in, and saw the great damage to the nation the paper "Continental Dollar" caused. Those men voted on and struck down the emission of paper money. They further limited the government's power over money. The Federal government was limited to coining money and regulating its value. They also provided that no state shall *make anything but gold and silver coin a tender in payment of debts.* (Art. 1, Sec. 10)

INFLATION 1800-1995

In spite of the fact that these constitutional provisions have never been officially or legally altered, in the year 1934 the Federal Government confiscated all of the gold money of its citizens and passed a law making it a criminal offense to use gold as money. (U.S.C. Title 31, Sec. 443) As of today (1967) the Federal government is in the final stages of removing all silver backing for its currency and has substituted base metals for silver and gold in its coins.

Thus, one more of the constitutional safeguards to the right of private property has been removed and the proposal of the Communists adopted. Today the Federal government has not only the power to borrow huge sums of money from its citizens and pay such debts with "printing press money," but it can destroy the creditor class by forcing them to accept a debauched and depreciated currency from other debtors in lieu of hard money which a redeemable currency provides.

We will not examine individually the last five points of the Manifesto. They call for centralized government control over communication, transportation, factories, farms, labor, and education. These proposals constitute an additional method of destroying private property by so regulating and regimenting the so-called owner in the use of it that he is owner in name only.

As originally interpreted, the United States Constitution denied government the right to regulate and control the citizen in the use of his property. Over the years the commerce clause and the general welfare clause have been so interpreted as to permit both the state and Federal governments to regiment labor, agriculture, manufacturing, transportation, communication, finance and all other forms of economic activity. Today, if there is any limit on the power of government to regulate, no one knows what that limit is.

After comparing these two systems of government, and noting the changes we have wrought in our constitutional form, who can deny that we have largely abandoned the Lord's plan for Satan's? In an editorial in the U.S. News and World Report of July 20, 1964, entitled: "Our Vanishing Constitution," David Lawrence, nationally known writer said:

> Only 175 years after our forefathers ordained the Constitution of the United states, the document has largely fallen into disuse...We can hardly believe our eyes, however, as we reread the provisions of the Constitution that have been torn to shreds by the autocratic action of a judicial oligarchy.

The words used by Mr. Lawrence to describe what has happened are extremely interesting in the view of a prophecy made by the late President John Taylor in 1879 which is recorded in *Journal of Discourses*, Vol. 21, p. 8 as follows:

> The day is not far distant when this nation will be shaken from center to circumference. And now, you may write it down, any of you, and I will prophesy it in the name of God...When the people shall have torn to shreds the Constitution of the United States the Elders of Israel will be found holding it up to the nations of the earth and proclaiming liberty.

Each Elder of the Church might well ask himself where he stands with respect to these two documents—whether he is upholding the Constitution or helping to tear it to shreds and replace it with the provisions of the Manifesto. We might also ask ourselves what kind of a position of authority we can expect to occupy in the next life if we line up on Satan's side in the battle for freedom here.

One method in wide use today by those who are attempting to destroy our constitutional form of government is to discredit the Constitution by maligning and impugning the motives of the founding fathers who established it. The farther away from the event we get, the more some men believe they know the personal characters of those men, and the more evil they detect in their purposes.

Latter-day Saints should beware that they neither believe nor spread these falsehoods. Anyone who desires to know the facts would do well to study original source material such as the writings of these men and statements made by their contemporaries. If he does so he will find such unimpeachable source material as the following statements by James Madison and Alexis de Tocqueville:

> But, whatever may be the judgement pronounced on the competency of the architects of the Constitution, or whatever may be the destiny of the edifice prepared by them, I feel it a duty to express my profound and solemn conviction, derived from my intimate opportunity of observing and appreciating the views of the Convention, collectively and individually, that there never was an assembly of men, charged with a great and arduous trust, who were more pure in their motives, or more exclusively or anxiously devoted to the object committed to them, than were the members of the Federal Convention of 1787. (James Madison, *Elliot's Debates*, Vol V, p. 122)

> The assembly which accepted the task of composing the second Constitution was small; but George Washington was its President, and it contained the finest minds and the noblest characters that had ever appeared in the New World. (de Tocqueville, *Democracy in America*, Vol. 1, p. 118 Walter A. Knopf, Inc. 1945)

Latter-day Saints who condemn the architects of the Constitution and the work of their hands are rejecting the words of their scriptures. The Lord has told us that these men were wise men; that

He raised them up for this very purpose, and that they acted under His inspiration. (D&C 101:77; D&C 109:54.)

Those who see selfish motives in the founding fathers for establishing a government which protected their own properties should realize that it would have been impossible for them to have government protect property rights in general without protecting their own. We have been told that no government can exist in peace unless the right and control of property is protected. (D&C 134:2) It is Satan's form of government which would destroy this basic human right so essential to freedom.

CHAPTER IX

THE "VOICE FROM THE DUST" SPEAKS TO MODERN AMERICA ABOUT GOVERNMENT

It appears that one of the main purposes of the Lord in giving us the Book of Mormon was to warn us against destroying ourselves through the adoption of Satan's form of government. Two mighty civilizations were destroyed on this land choice above all other lands and the cause of destruction was the same in each case—the corruption of government by wickedness.

Moroni, that servant of God through whom Joseph Smith received the Book of Mormon, was expressly commanded by the Lord to warn the Gentiles (us) against committing national suicide in this manner. Let us note his solemn warnings:

> And they (secret combinations) have caused the destruction of this people of whom I am now speaking, (Jaredites) and also the destruction of the people of Nephi... Wherefore, O ye Gentiles, it is wisdom in God that these things should be shown unto you, that thereby ye may repent of your sins, and suffer not that these murderous combinations shall get above you...Wherefore, the Lord commandeth you, when ye shall see these things come among you that ye shall awake to a sense of your awful situation,...Wherefore I, Moroni, am commanded to write these things. (Ether 8:21-26)

64

President McKay has identified Communism as this secret combination of Satan which threatens our very existence today. (*Statements on Communism and the Constitution of the United States*, p. 5)

He has also said:

> The position of this Church on the subject of Communism has never changed. We consider it the greatest satanical threat to peace, prosperity, and the spread of God's work among men that exists on the face of the earth....We therefore commend and encourage every person and every group who is sincerely seeking to study Constitutional principles and awaken a sleeping and apathetic people to the alarming conditions that are rapidly advancing about us. (*Improvement Era*, June 1966, p. 477)

The Lord, through Moroni, has commanded us to awaken. The Lord, through our living prophet, has indicated we are still asleep. Is it not time we listen to the Lord? Our destruction as a nation is certain unless we do:

> And whatsoever nation shall uphold such secret combinations, to get power and gain, until they shall spread over the nation, behold, they shall be destroyed. (Ether 8:22)

Let us briefly examine the Nephite experience with a government subject to the voice of the people to see what lessons it might teach.

It is rare in the history of nations when the Lord gives a people the power to determine for themselves what civil laws they shall be subject to and who shall execute those laws. For over 500 years the Nephites lived under a monarchy and then about 125 years before Christ's visit to them, He caused to be established among them a new type of government similar to the one He caused to be set up in the United States 180 years ago.

There appear to be some important differences between the Nephite government called the *reign of the judges* and our own, yet this they had in common: both were subject to control by the voice of the people.

When King Mosiah effected this change under the Lord's direction, the Nephites were told, just as we have been told, that they would be held individually accountable for the actions of their government. The people seemed to sense their responsibility for the record says:

> Therefore they relinquished their desires for a king, and became exceedingly anxious that every man should have an equal chance throughout all the land; yea, and every man expressed a willingness to answer for his own sins. (Mosiah 29:38)

The Nephites were told that if they abused this new freedom to control government, the Lord would punish them. They were instructed thus:

> Now it is not common that the voice of the people desireth anything contrary to that which is right; but it is common for the lesser part of the people to desire that which is not right; therefore this shall ye observe and make it your law—to do your business by the voice of the people. And if the time comes that the voice of the people doth choose iniquity, then is the time that the judgments of God will come upon you; yea, then is the time he will visit you with great destruction even as he has hitherto visited this land. (Mosiah 29:26-27)

Some 62 years after the reign of the judges was established, the Nephites had corrupted their government, and conditions were so bad that Nephi, a righteous prophet and the Chief Judge, resigned his position because he was weary of the people's iniquity and wished to spend his full time calling them to repentance. The political situation is described by the record as follows:

> For as their laws and their governments were established by the voice of the people, and they who chose evil were more numerous than they who chose good, therefore they were ripening for destruction, for the laws had become corrupted. (Helaman 5:2)

In the next chapter (6) of the record we are given to understand how this corruption took place. The Gadianton Band had arisen among the Nephites about twenty years prior to this and increased in size and influence until, at this time, even the righteous believed in its philosophy of government and accepted its practices. The record says:

> And it came to pass on the other hand, that the Nephites did build them (Gadianton Band) up and support them, beginning at the more wicked part of them, until they had overspread all the land of the Nephites, and had seduced the more part of the righteous until they had come down to believe in their works and partake of their spoils, and to join with them in their secret murders and combinations. (Helaman 6:38)

Having corrupted everyone with their doctrines, this Gadianton Band *did obtain the sole management of the government.* (Helaman 6:39) Nephi, the prophet who had been in the land northward preaching, returned to the land of Zarahemla to find:

> ...those Gadianton robbers filling the judgment-seats— having usurped the power and authority of the land; laying aside the commandments of God,...Condemning the righteous because of their righteousness; letting the guilty and the wicked go unpunished because of their money; and moreover to be held in office at the head of government, to rule and do according to their wills, that they might get gain and glory of the world, and, moreover, that they might the more easily commit adultery, and steal, and kill, and do according to their own wills...(Helaman 7:4-5)

It may seem incredible that the righteous Nephites could have been seduced into accepting the doctrines and practices of a group which the Nephite prophets called *robbers.* How blind can people be? Before we judge them too harshly let us look at our own predicament.

Every modern day prophet from Joseph Smith to President McKay has condemned Communism and Socialism as satanic systems of plunder by government, and yet how many Latter-day Saints have come down to accept and believe in those very welfare state practices which the Communist Manifesto proposes to bring about socialism? How many believe in and accept the government bonus, the subsidy, the welfare check, the minimum wage, and the monopolistic protection which the police power gives them? Is it not obvious that we also have come down to believe in their works and partake of their spoils?

There is evidence that the Gadianton Robbers proposed exactly the same form of government as do the Communists today. The Nephite prophet, Mormon, saw fit to copy into the record an epistle written by Giddianhi, Governor of the Gadianton Band, to Lachoneus, Governor of the Nephites, in which are some very revealing statements. This letter is found in 3 Nephi, Chapter 3. Verse 7 thereof indicates that the Gadianton Band believed in communal ownership of property. In that verse Giddianhi says to Lachoneus:

> Or in other words, yield yourselves up unto us, and unite with us and become acquainted with our secret works, and become our brethren that ye may be like unto us—not our slaves, but our brethren and partners of all our substance.

What could he have meant by the expression *partners of all our substance* except communal ownership of property?

Giddianhi also accuses the Nephites of robbing his people of *their rights and government.* (v. 10) This is the identical appeal which the Communists make to the laboring class today. They appeal to their selfishness and tell them they are exploited and robbed under the capitalistic system and are denied their rights of government. The Communists propose the establishment of what they call the *dictatorship of proletariat* whereunder the workers are supposed to own all the property and run the government. One can hardly imagine a greater deception than this but it is the appeal made nonetheless.

Giddianhi also speaks of the *everlasting hatred* (v. 4) of his people for the Nephites. V.I. Lenin, first Communist dictator in Russia and one of the chief theoreticians of Communism had this to say:

We must hate. Hatred is the basis of Communism. Children must be taught to hate their parents if they are not Communists.

Throughout Giddianhi's epistle runs a threat to exterminate the Nephites if they do not *Yield up unto this my people, your cities, your lands, and your possessions.* (v. 6) How typical this is of the Communist leaders today who arrogantly proclaim to the capitalist world: *We will bury you.*

The underlying purposes of the Gadianton Band were described by Mormon thus:

> ...it was the object of all those who belonged to his (Gadianton's) band to murder, and to rob, and to gain power, (and this was their secret plan, and their combination)...(Helaman 2:8)

But the power they sought and the opportunity to carry on their work of plunder and murder could be fully obtained only by taking over and controlling the agency of government. This was their unvarying goal. During an 82 year period they murdered the Chiefs of State of the Nephite nation five times and made one additional unsuccessful attempt.

In the one instance where they did succeed in taking over the reigns of government, it was through a combination of murder and seducing the people to partake of their spoils with them. The prophet Moroni thoroughly understood the nature of these secret combinations. In his warning to the Gentiles against them he says:

> For it cometh to pass that whoso buildeth it (secret combinations) up seeketh to overthrow the freedom of all lands, nations, and countries... (Ether 8:25)

Can anyone give a more accurate description than that of the Communist movement today? Its avowed purpose is to overthrow every non-communist government on earth and establish a world-wide dictatorship.

J. Edgar Hoover, director of the F.B.I., and one of the best informed men on Communism, has said this:

The communist is thinking in terms of now, in your lifetime. Remember that within four decades communism, as a state power, has spread through roughly 40 percent of the earth's surface. Some years ago communists were complaining that their 'fatherland,' Soviet Russia, was encircled, a communist island in a 'capitalist' sea. Today the situation is changed. The world communist movement is on the march, into Germany, the Balkans, the Middle East, stretching across the plains of Asia into China, Korea, and Indochina. Communists have never hesitated to shed blood if this would best serve their purposes. Moreover, in noncommunist countries thousands of Party members are working for Moscow. Communists firmly believe they are destined to conquer the world. (J. Edgar Hoover, *Masters of Deceit*, p. 4 Henry Holt & Co., Inc. 1958)

The deadly parallel between the purposes and methods of the Secret Combinations of old and the Communist conspiracy of today is plain for all to see. It is interesting to observe that the Communists even use the word *combination* to describe their activities. Note the following passage taken from the book, *Witness*, authored by the late ex-communist, Whittaker Chambers:

One story…sheds light on the more menacing operations of the underground. It was the story of how the Russians obtained data about the Chrystie tank. This tank, developed by the American inventor, Walter Chrystie, was of great interest to the Russians. They set on foot an elaborate 'combination' (as Communists call it) to secure its plans. (Whittaker Chambers, *Witness*, p. 319. Random House, 1952)

When the Secret Combination among the Nephites finally succeeded in capturing control of their government, civil strife broke out and threatened to destroy the nation by bloodshed. (Helaman 11:2-4) The prophet Nephi pled with the Lord to send a famine to humble the people rather than permitting them to destroy each other by the sword. This was done. Thousands died of starvation. The people were brought to a realization of their wickedness and swept the Gadianton Band from their government. The Lord turned away His wrath and sent rain upon the earth.

It was but a short space of time, however, before many of the people reverted to wickedness. The Gadianton Band formed again. This time, however, it appears that the righteous people refused to be seduced into perverting their government with welfare state practices. Their recent experience was too fresh upon their minds. There occurred a great division among the people, the Gadianton Robbers forming one group, the more righteous Nephites and Lamanites banding together in another. A terrible battle ensued between these opponents which produced the greatest slaughter ever known among the children of Lehi since he left Jerusalem. (3 Nephi 4:11) The Nephite-Lamanite armies conquered and once again this terrible conspiracy was crushed.

After another brief period of righteousness, the people again became wicked. For the third time the Robbers became a threat to the continued existence of orderly government. In this third instance, the Gadianton Band did succeed in destroying organized government by murdering the chief judge. The people, unable to reconstitute a supreme government, formed themselves into tribes.

The Robbers failed in this bid to take over the Nephite government because they were inferior in numbers to the tribes who:

> ...notwithstanding they were not a righteous people, yet
> they were united in the hatred of those who had entered into
> a covenant to destroy the government. (3 Ne. 7:11)

The Robbers left the main body of the Nephites and went into the land northward. They hoped to gather strength enough to return and conquer.

It was at this point in Nephite history that Christ visited them. All the wicked were destroyed in that terrible cataclysm of fire and the upheavals of nature. Christ had an especially severe judgement which He inflicted upon this criminal group of conspirators who had destroyed the Nephite government. He describes their fate in 3 Ne. 9:9:

> And behold, that great city Jacobugath, which was
> inhabited by the people of King Jacob, have I caused to be

71

burned with fire because of their sins and their wickedness, which was above all the wickedness of the whole earth, because of their secret murders and combinations; for it was they that did destroy the peace of my people and the government of the land.

Thus ended the first Nephite experience with a government by the voice of the people.

Following the visit of Christ, the Nephites lived in peace and righteousness for almost 200 years. When they became wicked, however, we find this same criminal conspiracy among them. (4 Ne. 42) The record is sketchy during this period. We are told that the Robbers were at the bargaining table when a great division of the land was made between the Nephites and the Lamanites. (Mormon 2:28) As noted heretofore, Secret Combinations were the cause of the eventual and final destruction of the Nephites as well as of the nation of Jaredites.

The Bible is, for the most part, a history of God's dealings with man in the *old world,* whereas the Book of Mormon was written by prophets in the Americas and its messages are directed primarily to those who inhabit this land. One lesson, in particular, which must be learned by those who come here is this: We must serve God or be destroyed.

The Book of Mormon prophets repeat this unalterable decree of God many times. The histories of those two great civilizations who rose and fell here provide instructive examples of the enforcement of this decree. The first people to arrive here after the Lord had cleansed the earth with water were the Jaredites. The warning issued to them through their first leader is as follows:

> And he (God) had sworn in his wrath unto the brother of Jared, that whoso should possess this land of promise, from that time henceforth and forever, should serve him, the true and only God, or they should be swept off when the fullness of his wrath should come upon them. (Ether 2:8)

The Jaredite nation occupied this chosen land for approximately two thousand years before they *became fully ripe in iniquity* and were swept off. About the time of their destruction, the Lord brought another group, the Nephites, here and through their first prophet, Lehi, warned them:

Wherefore, this land is consecrated unto him whom he (God) shall bring. And if it so be that they shall serve him according to the commandments which he hath given, it shall be a land of liberty unto them; wherefore, they shall never be brought down into captivity; if so, it shall be because of iniquity; for if iniquity shall abound cursed shall be the land for their sakes, but unto the righteous it shall be blessed forever. (2 Nephi 1:7)

Not long after the Nephites arrived, the Lord placed in their hands the record of the Jaredites, and brought to their attention the ruins of that civilization so that they might have before them an object lesson. The Nephite prophets reminded their people of the destruction of the Jaredite nation from time to time. In spite of their knowledge that secret combinations had caused it, the Nephites allowed these same organizations to arise among them, and this was the cause of their eventual destruction.

We, the Gentiles, constitute a third group who have been favored to occupy this chosen land. To those of us living under the Constitution established by the Lord, it has proved to be a choice land almost beyond belief. With approximately six percent of the world's population, we are reputed to have over one half of the world's wealth. Our great blessings will be followed by equally great cursings if we, as a nation, turn from God. The book of Mormon is very explicit about this:

And this cometh unto you, O ye Gentiles, that ye may know the decrees of God—that ye may repent, and not continue in your iniquities until the fullness come, that ye may not bring down the fullness of the wrath of God upon you as the inhabitants of the land have hitherto done. (Ether 2:11)

Let us consider in connection with the above scripture an admonition given in our day regarding our failure to heed the lessons of the Book of Mormon. The Lord has placed the entire Church under condemnation and told us we would remain there until we hearken to the commandments in that book:

And your minds in times past have been darkened because of unbelief, and because you have treated lightly the things you have received-which vanity and unbelief have brought the whole church under condemnation. And this condemnation resteth upon the children of Zion, even all. And they shall remain under this condemnation until they repent and remember the new covenant, even the Book of Mormon and the former commandments which I have given them, not only to say but to do according to that which I have written. (D&C 84:54-57)

In the two verses which follow the above statement, the Lord tells us that if we corrupt His holy land, a judgment and a scourge will be poured out upon us:

That they may bring forth fruit meet for their Father's kingdom; otherwise there remaineth a scourge and judgement to be poured our upon the children of Zion. For shall the children of the kingdom pollute my holy land? Verily, I say unto you, Nay. (D&C 84:58-59)

That we are in the process of polluting this land is plain for all to see. Nowhere is it more apparent than in our laws and our governments. The corruption of the principles of the Constitution by the adoption of the welfare state practices advocated by the Communists has been pointed out herein. Our living prophet in his recent statement concerning the position of the Church on Communism has warned us. He speaks of the *alarming conditions that are rapidly advancing about us.* Those cannot be misinterpreted by anyone willing to listen.

The Lord's admonition to us through Moroni is equally plain:

Wherefore, the Lord commandeth you, when ye shall see these things come among you that ye shall awake to a sense of your awful situation, because of this secret combination which shall be among you. (Ether 8:24)

CHAPTER X

SPECIFIC LESSONS FROM THE NEPHITE RECORD

Perhaps the Nephite scriptures can aid us in seeing more clearly where the path of political duty lies. One outstanding example of a righteous man acting with the approval of the Lord in a political and military capacity to preserve the liberty of the people is that of the general, Moroni.

In the 19th year of the reign of the judges, Amalickiah, an extremely wicked Nephite, sought to destroy the freedom of the nation by corrupting the lower judges and making himself king. He undoubtedly would have succeeded had not Moroni raised his *title of liberty* and gone throughout the land rallying the people to the support of free government. Moroni overcame the opposition of Amalickiah and put to death those of his followers who denied the covenant of freedom.

A few years later a political group called *kingmen* were defeated at the polls. They too, attempted to change the government to a monarchy by majority vote. Angered at their failure, they refused to join in the defense of the nation against an enemy invasion. Moroni led his armies against these rebels, and executed some 4,000 of them. He compelled those who were not put to death or imprisoned, to hoist the title of liberty on their towers.

Moroni literally gave his life for the cause of freedom. He became supreme commander of the Nephite armies at the age of 25; served in that capacity through a terrible period of warfare for 14 years, and died 5 years after he had retired, at the age of 43. This *strong and mighty man* must have exerted himself to the uttermost limit in the defense of his country. His magnificent service brought the following words of praise from Mormon, the historian:

> And Moroni was a strong and a mighty man; he was a man of a perfect understanding; yea, a man that did not delight in bloodshed; a man whose soul did joy in the liberty and the freedom of his country, and his brethren from bondage and slavery;
>
> Yea, and he was a man who was firm in the faith of Christ, and he had sworn with an oath to defend his people, his rights, and his country, and his religion, even to the loss of his blood.
>
> Yea, verily, verily I say unto you, if all men had been, and were, and ever would be like unto Moroni, behold, the very powers of hell would have been shaken forever; yea, the devil would never have power over the hearts of the children of men. (Alma 48:11, 13, 17)

Few men, if any, have ever been lauded by a prophet of God in such extravagant terms. And who can doubt but that he was most deserving? Insofar as the record tells us, he never held a position of any prominence in the Church, but his "political" and "military" services were as vital to the work of the Lord as were the efforts of the prophets. (Alma 48:18-19)

Suppose that he had stayed comfortably and safely at home performing his "regular church duties" rather than going throughout the land on his political campaign. Or suppose that the prophet Helaman had confined himself strictly to preaching the word rather than leading his 2,000 stripling soldiers to war, thus preventing the collapse of the western battle front. In either case the Nephites would have lost their freedom, and the Church of Christ would have been destroyed.

The Nephite prophets took an extremely active part in the political activities of their nation during the reign of the judges. The people had the privilege of selecting by majority vote their officers of government and, more often than not, the person chosen by the people to serve as governor over all the land was also head of the church.

Not only did these prophets serve in political positions but as military leaders as well. The record tells us:

> Now it was the custom among all the Nephites to appoint for their chief captains, (save it were in their times of wickedness) some one that had the spirit of revelation and also prophesy. (3 Nephi 3:19)

When the Nephites corrupted the laws which the Lord had given them, these religious leaders spoke out boldly against such corruption. They did so with the Lord's approval:

> For behold, Nephi had spoken unto them concerning the corruptness of their law; yea, many things did Nephi speak which cannot be written; and nothing did he speak which was contrary to the commandments of God. (Helaman 8:3)

When there was iniquity among those in political office the prophets did not hesitate to point this out and warn the people that such unrighteousness by their rulers would cause their destruction. Amulek spoke to the people of Ammonihah thus:

> And now behold, I say unto you, that the foundation of the destruction of this people is beginning to be laid by the unrighteousness of your lawyers and your judges. (Alma 10:27)

The record is clear that these prophets risked their lives when they uttered such criticisms, but this did not deter them.

It is of course recognized that some men are better equipped to preach than to fight or occupy positions of power and influence in government. The Nephite record also teaches us that when the people become exceedingly corrupt, a righteous man better serves God by preaching than governing. Note for example the resignations of both Alma and Nephi from the top position in government so that they could spend their full time calling the people to repentance. (Alma 4:18; Helaman 5:4)

77

The Nephite experience with a government by the voice of the people makes it clear that in addition to the usual duty of Church members to protect their God-given freedoms, in times of great peril extreme measures may be necessary. In a period of crisis, total sacrifice may be required.

President McKay has told us we are now in one of those periods of crisis. He has identified the nature of that crisis beyond any doubt. The frightening fact is that the satanic movement of which he warns is the same which caused the destruction of the other civilizations which occupied this land.

Those Nephite prophets who tried vainly to prevent the destruction of their nation were also commanded by the Lord to warn us. They prophesied that we would face the same threat. They supplied us with a rather detailed history of how this criminal conspiracy operates to destroy a nation whose government is subject to the voice of the people.

It is a point of some interest that while the Jaredite nation existed on this chosen land approximately twice as long as the Nephites and was the greater nation, still the Book of Mormon is about 94% Nephite history with only 32 pages devoted to that nation about which the Lord told the brother of Jared:

> There shall be none greater than the nation which I will raise up unto me of thy seed, upon all the face of the earth. (Ether 1:43)

It is probable that the reason the Jaredite history is slighted in favor of that of the Nephites is that the latter lived a part of their time under a government similar to the one the Lord gave us. This probability is strengthened by the fact that while the Nephite history covers about 1,000 years, almost one-half of that portion of their record placed in our hands concerns that brief 125 year period during which the people tried to govern themselves by majority vote.

Of extreme importance to us, it would seem, are those particulars concerning how, during this period of self-government, the Nephites subjected themselves to the criminal conspiracy. It destroyed their government. Our prophet tells us it threatens ours. Let us examine some of the details of that occurrence and compare them with what is happening in our own nation.

Of particular significance is the fact that they had altered and corrupted the laws God had given them. This was done with the consent of the majority of the people:

> And that they had altered and trampled under their feet the laws of Mosiah, or that which the Lord commanded him to give unto the people...For as their laws and their governments were established by the voice of the people, and they who chose evil were more numerous than they who chose good, therefore they were ripening for destruction for the laws had become corrupted. (Hel. 4:22; 5:2)

How have we treated that Constitution which the Lord caused to be established among us? The extent to which we have altered it and substituted therefor the proposals of the Communist Manifesto has been discussed herein. Our modern prophets continue to warn us that we are corrupting our laws. President McKay said back in 1952:

> During the first half of the twentieth century we have traveled far into the soul-destroying land of socialism... (*Gospel Ideals*, p. 273)

Those interested in reading some of the numerous statements made by President McKay and other Church leaders on the subject of Communism and the threat it poses to our government would do well to study the booklet, *Statements on Communism and the Constitution of the United States*, Deseret Book Co., 1966, and the book, *Prophets, Principles and National Survival*, by Jerreld L. Newquist, Publishers Press, 1964.

Another factor in the takeover of the Nephite government which should have great meaning to us is that the people were seduced or deceived into believing in the philosophy of government espoused by the Gadianton Band:

> ...the Nephites did build them (the Gadianton Band) up and support them, beginning at the more wicked part of them, until they had overspread all the land of the Nephites, and had seduced the more part of the righteous until they had

come down to believe in their works and partake of their spoils,… (Hel. 6:38)

Back in 1940, the First Presidency of the Church issued a statement on Communism in which they said:

We again warn our people in America of the constantly increasing threat against our inspired Constitution…These revolutionists are using a technique that is as old as the human race—a fervid but false solicitude for the unfortunate over whom they thus gain mastery, and then enslave them…Latter-day Saints cannot be true to their faith and lend aid, encouragement, or sympathy to any of these false philosophies. They will prove snares to their feet. (David O. McKay, *Statements on Communism and the Constitution of the United States*, pp. 7-8)

It is obvious that these secret combinations (robbers by government) have not changed their tactics since the days of the Nephites. When the power of government is placed in the hands of the people, the conspirators appeal to our selfishness. They seduce us to *partake of their spoils* of government until they enslave us.

It was by such deceit and bribery that the Gadianton Band *did obtain the sole management of the government*. The Nephites, by majority vote, had elected to office men who believed in robbery by government. The prophet Nephi, returning from the land northward found:

…the people in a state of such awful wickedness, and those Gadianton robbers filling the judgment-seats—having usurped the power and authority of the land…(Hel. 7:4)

The statement of David Lawrence which appears elsewhere in this work wherein he refers to, the *provisions of the Constitution that have been torn to shreds by the autocratic action of a judicial oligarchy*, takes on added significance when considered in the light of a similar usurpation of power and authority by the Nephite judges.

Having been commanded by the Lord to do so, Nephi boldly told the people that they had united themselves to this band of robbers:

> Yea, wo be unto you because of that great abomination which has come among you; and ye have united yourselves unto it, yea to that secret band which was established by Gadianton! (Hel. 7:25)

One can imagine that those righteous Nephites who had been *seduced* into upholding, supporting, and partaking of the spoils of the Robbers were profoundly shocked when charged with having united with a criminal conspiracy. People in our nation today are ofttimes startled and angered when told that the welfare state practices they favor are the identical political programs proposed by the Communists to bring about socialism.

There were, in Nephi's audience, some men who actually belonged to the conspiracy:

> ...there were men who were judges, who also belonged to the secret band of Gadianton, and they were angry...(Hel. 8:1)

And why were they angry? Nephi had exposed them. He pointed out the corruption of the laws had resulted in the takeover of the Nephite government by this Band:

> For behold, Nephi had spoken unto them concerning the corruptness of their law...And those judges were angry with him because he spake plainly unto them concerning their secret works of darkness. (Hel. 8:3-4)

The record is clear that the reason the conspiracy had succeeded in capturing control of the government was that the Nephites had built it up and supported it and had been seduced into partaking of its spoils. (Hel. 6:38-39)

The great majority of the people today continue to ignore the prophets' warnings that the advance of Communism within our own nation is leading us to destruction. Likewise, the Nephites ignored their prophet:

> And it came to pass that they would not hearken unto his words; and there began to be contentions, insomuch that they were divided against themselves and began to slay one another with the sword. (Hel. 10:18)

> And it was this secret band of robbers who did carry on this work of destruction and wickedness…(Hel. 11:2)

The unmistakable parallel between the Communist inspired rioting, looting, burning, and bloodshed in our own cities which increase each year, and the bloody turmoil among the Nephites should cause us great anxiety. It is noted that the Nephites divided against themselves and began to kill one another. Who will deny that there is a rift in our own nation which becomes more pronounced as the Communist programs to centralize the powers of government and destroy the right of private property continue to be adopted and expanded?

The Lord brought an end to the bloodshed among the Nephites and released their nation from the clutches of this conspiracy by means of a great drought and famine. Will He prevent this nation from destroying itself in a civil war by the same means? If so, He probably would not need to send a drought to do it. With continued internal strife, we could bring about our own famine, and do it very suddenly.

With less than ten percent of our population engaged in farming, and with this small group almost completely dependent upon a continuing supply of fuel, machinery, and a smoothly functioning transportation network, famine could and would stalk the land within a matter of weeks if violence interrupted the operation of this highly interdependent system of food production and distribution.

Perhaps no people in history have been as vulnerable to starvation as is this nation today. Highly specialized in our labor, and relying almost completely upon electric power and labor-saving machinery, we have largely forgotten the meaning of physical labor and the art of feeding and clothing ourselves. If our power supply, our production machinery, or our transportation facilities were to break down, food markets would empty within hours and people would be left to their own devices to provide themselves with sustenance. The massiveness of the tragedy which could result is horrible to contemplate. While the Nephites perished by the thousands, we would likely starve by the millions.

We have facing us a danger even more fearful, if possible, than those which faced the Nephites. This is the threat of a nuclear war. A few days after he was made President of the Church, David O. McKay said:

> A third World War is inevitable unless Communism is soon subdued. Communism yields to nothing but force. (*Statements on Communism and the Constitution of the United States,* p. 13)

It seems to be a foregone conclusion that such a war will develop into a nuclear holocaust. The Lord has permitted the world to have a foretaste of the horrors of such an eventuality, but since Hiroshima and Nagasaki, the destructiveness of nuclear weapons has multiplied many times.

The exact nature, however, of the calamities which may befall us, whether they be civil war, famine, international nuclear war, or otherwise, is relatively unimportant. The important fact is the inevitability of the destruction of this nation from some source unless we heed the words of the prophets.

It must be most disheartening to a prophet to know with certainty that the nation and people he loves are marching steadily toward their doom and be unable to dissuade them. When Nephi failed to get his nation to listen, he was so deeply distressed that he lamented the fact that he could not have lived his days in a period of time when the people would hearken. (Hel. 7:7) He was so cast down at his failure that the Lord saw fit to personally comfort him. (Hel. 10:3-11)

One wonders at the feelings of our own Prophet as we continue to ignore his oft-repeated warnings against Communism and the moral breakdown which has caused us to adopt its philosophy. He continues to labor with us and his words are widely disseminated throughout the land just as were Nephi's warnings to his people.

CHAPTER XI

THE RESPONSIBILITY OF LATTER-DAY SAINTS

Latter-day Saints are the only people who have been given an understanding of the exact nature of the predicament we are in. We alone know that God through His mouthpiece has told us we are in dire peril. The responsibility to act has been placed upon us. The blessings of the gospel do not come without equivalent duties. Our failure to assume them will bring severe condemnation:

> For of him unto whom much is given much is required; and he who sins against the greater light shall receive the greater condemnation. (D&C 82:3)

If we sit idly by, unmoved by the special knowledge which has been given, we are told our state will be awful:

> But wo unto him that has the law given, yea, that has all the commandments of God, like unto us, and that transgresseth them, and that wasteth the days of his probation, for awful is his state. (2 Ne. 9:27)

Latter-day Saints have been directed to give heed to the Lord's commandments concerning the laws of the land:

And now, verily I say unto you concerning the laws of the land, it is my will that my people should observe to do all things whatsoever I command them. (D&C 98:4)

We have been told to support that law of the land which is constitutional and not tamper with it:

Therefore, I, the Lord, justify you, and your brethren of my church, in befriending that law which is the constitutional law of the land; and as pertaining to law of man, whatsoever is more or less than this, cometh of evil. (D&C 98:6-7)

We have been advised to diligently seek for honest and wise men for our political leaders:

Nevertheless, when the wicked rule the people mourn. Wherefore honest men and wise men should be sought for diligently, and good men and wise men ye should observe to uphold; otherwise whatsoever is less than these cometh of evil. (D&C 98:9-10)

The Lord's commandments to us concerning our responsibilities to preserve the government which He caused to be established are just as binding as any other commandments of the gospel. It was necessary for the Lord to establish a government of freedom before He could restore His Church to the earth and establish it in this land. (3 Ne. 21:4) Is it not equally necessary to preserve that government so that His Church may remain here to perform its mission?

Immediately following the Lord's instructions in Section 98 to observe His commandments concerning the laws of the land, support the Constitution, and seek wise political leaders, we find this admonition:

And I give unto you a commandment,...that ye shall live by every word which proceedeth forth out of the mouth of God. (D&C 98:11)

It is entirely possible that the Lord is here pointedly reminding us that His instructions concerning the laws of the land are also a part of

His words, and they are not to be overlooked. Who can deny that Latter-day Saints need this reminding? How many of us are forming our political convictions by studying the scriptures? How many of us are even aware that the Lord has given extensive instructions regarding government?

On the other hand how many of us are getting our beliefs about government from books, magazines, newspapers, etc., written by men of the world with little or no regard to what the Lord has said? Do we know the penalty for hearkening to the precepts of men? Note these words of Nephi taken from his prophecies regarding the days of the Gentiles:

> ...they have all gone astray save it be a few, who are the humble followers of Christ; nevertheless, they are led, that in many instances they do err because they are taught by the precepts of men.
>
> Cursed is he that putteth his trust in man, or maketh flesh his arm, or shall hearken unto the precepts of men, save their precepts shall be given by the power of the Holy Ghost. (2 Ne. 28:14, 31)

Before we can obey God's commandments regarding the laws of the land we must know what those commandments are. This means we must search the scriptures. We must read them with the desire of finding the correct answers. We must test the philosophies of men by the revealed word of God or, according to Nephi, we will be cursed.

Not only must we study the scriptures, but as times and conditions change necessitating additional revelations, we must give heed when the Lord speaks through His living Mouthpiece.

One of the clearest and most recent admonitions of our prophet was given to the Priesthood of the Church at General Conference on April 9, 1966. In his Statement concerning the position of the Church on Communism, president McKay was quite specific about our failings and our responsibilities. He told us we are a sleeping and apathetic people. He spoke of the alarming conditions that are rapidly advancing about us. He encouraged us to study the Constitution and to become informed on the subject of Communism so that we could better appreciate what is happening and know what (we) can do about it. He described Communism as the greatest satanical threat on earth, and told us that if we, as Church members and American citizens, lent aid, encouragement, or sympathy to any of these false philosophies they would prove snares to our feet.

JOHN TAYLOR

I was speaking, a while ago, about the people there being divided into three classes. One of them you may call infidel, under the head of socialism, fourierism, and several other isms. Communism is a specimen of the same thing,.. (John Taylor, *Journal of Discourses,* Vol. 1, p. 23, August 22, 1852)

HEBER J. GRANT

...this we feel we can definitely say, that unless the people of America forsake the sins and the errors, political and otherwise, of which they are now guilty and return to the practice of the great fundamental principles of Christianity, and of Constitutional government, there will be no exaltation for them spiritually, and politically we shall lose our liberty and free institutions.

We believe that our real threat comes from within and not from without, and it comes from the underlying spirit common to Naziism, Fascism, and Communism, namely, the spirit which would array class against class, which would set up a socialistic state of some sort, which would rob the people of the liberties which we possess under the Constitution, and would set up such a reign of terror as exists now in many parts of Europe....

Faithfully yours, /s/ *Heber J. Grant, J. Reuben Clark, Jr., David O. McKay.* (First Presidency letter to U.S. Treasury, September 30, 1941)

GEORGE ALBERT SMITH

As one man said to me, "Why not try what Russia has tried and what Germany has tried?" And my answer to him was, "Why try something that has already failed? Why not hold on to what the Lord has given?" *(The Teachings of George Albert Smith,* Bookcraft, Salt Lake City, [1996], p. 171)

CHAPTER XII

SUMMARY

The words of the prophets, ancient and modern, seem to have left us with these alternatives: As a nation we face temporal and spiritual destruction and captivity unless we repent and serve the God of this land, cleanse our governments of those practices of Communism we have adopted, and return to the God-given principles of freedom established by our Founding Fathers. (1 Ne. 14:7; Ether 2:9-12; Ether 8:22-24) As a Church we have been placed under condemnation and it appears that we will lose those blessings and Priesthood Powers infinitely more valuable than any earthly sacrifice, unless we heed the words of the prophets, completely reject the Satan-inspired philosophy of exercising unrighteous dominion through government, and sacrifice our time, means, and life, if necessary, to preserve the freedoms and the religion God has given us. (D&C 84:54-59; D&C 121:34, 40)

In the early days of our Church, many Saints gave up their friends and loved ones, their possessions, and even their lives that the gospel might remain upon the earth. The Church was forced to flee into the wilderness to escape the intense religious bigotry and hate directed against it.

Politically inspired hatred and bigotry can be equally as intense. The time foreseen by Nephi (I Ne. 14:12-13) when the Lamb of God would stand alone against the Mother of Abominations may now be at hand. Satan's form of Government, Communism, and those political systems which lead to it—Welfare Statism and Socialism— have now spread over the earth. A period of bitter persecution

89

against those who resist these movements is only to be expected. The Prophet Joseph Smith has written:

> ...the destinies of all people are in the hands of a just God, and He will do no injustice to any one; and this one thing is sure, that they who will live godly in Christ Jesus, shall suffer persecution; and before their robes are made white in the blood of the Lamb, it is to be expected, according to John the Revelator, they will pass through great tribulation. (*History of the Church*, Vol. 1, p. 449)

President McKay has issued a call to the Saints to sacrifice on behalf of their religious, political, and economic freedoms which are threatened by welfare state practices. Consider his words carefully:

> No greater immediate responsibility rests upon members of the Church, upon all citizens of this Republic and of neighboring Republics, than to protect the freedom vouchsafed by the Constitution of the United States.
>
> Let us, by exercising our privileges under the Constitution—
>
> (1) Preserve our right to worship God according to the dictates of our conscience.
>
> (2) Preserve the right to work when and where we choose. No free man should be compelled to pay tribute in order to realize this God-given privilege.
>
> Read in the Doctrine and Covenants this statement:
> ...it is not right that any man should be in bondage one to another. (D&C 101:79)
>
> (3) Feel free to plant and to reap without the handicap of bureaucratic interference.
>
> (4) Devote our time, means, and life if necessary, to hold inviolate those laws which will secure to each individual the free exercise of conscience, the right and control of property, and the protection of life. (David O. McKay, *Statements on Communism and the Constitution of the United States*, 1966, pp. 11-12)

Perhaps never before in the history of the world has there been a greater need and a greater opportunity for fighting the battle of freedom. The weapon with which this battle must be fought and won—the truth—is in our hands. God has placed it there. He has also provided us with many miraculous devices for wielding this weapon. We have at our disposal a marvelous variety of communication facilities.

Every Latter-day Saint should thoroughly understand the fact that Satan's great weapon today is political in nature. The religion which he is effectively espousing is the destruction of free agency by destroying the right and control of property; it is robbery by government. We should know from what our prophets have told us that Communism, Socialism, and Welfare Statism are each a part of this satanic doctrine.

Knowing these vital truths, we have an immense and urgent responsibility to share this God-given knowledge with others and to use every means available to combat Satan's plan for our destruction as a Nation and as a Church.

Should we not assume our immediate responsibility? Should we not give of our time and means, and speak out while this course remains open to us? Shall we wait until it becomes necessary to sacrifice our lives for the preservation of freedom, as our prophet has indicated may become necessary?

The Book of Mormon prophets have been very plain in telling us that the same threat we face today caused their extinction. Satan induced them to use their governments as a tool of self-destruction. The Secret Combinations and Gadianton Robbers had the same objective as Communism does today: to seize control of government and then use it to rob, to murder, and to enslave.

The voices from the dust are pleading with us not to repeat the tragic history of their people. You and I are to face those men at the judgment bar of God where their words will condemn us if we fail to heed their warnings. Listen and you can hear them speaking to you:

> And now, beloved brethren, all those who are of the house of Israel, and all ye ends of the earth, I speak unto you as the voice of one crying from the dust: Farewell until that great day shall come.

91

And you that will not partake of the goodness of God, and respect the words of the Jews, and also my words, and the words which shall proceed forth out of the mouth of the Lamb of God, behold, I bid you an everlasting farewell, for these words shall condemn you at the last day.

For what I seal on earth, shall be brought against you at the judgment bar; for thus hath the Lord commanded me, and I must obey. Amen. (2 Ne. 33:13-15)

And now I speak unto all the ends of the earth for the time speedily cometh that I lie not, for ye shall see me at the bar of God; and the Lord God will say unto you: Did I not declare my words unto you, which were written by this man, like as one crying from the dead, yea, even as one speaking out of the dust? (Mor. 10:24, 27)

PRESIDENT THOMAS S. MONSON

Of all the individuals I know, who would like to be here today, it would be Ezra Taft Benson, the Prophet of the Lord, and the President of the Church. For, he loved Verlan Andersen, and he loves all of us...

As I describe my friend Verlan, I would like to say that he was a man of integrity. When he knew he was right, he followed it. There was no discussion. There was no temptation...

Verlan Andersen never endorsed that with which he did not agree, for he wanted to be able to defend his position, and his position was always on the side of the Lord.

He truly was a man of integrity...

(President Thomas S. Monson, speaking at the funeral of Elder H. Verlan Andersen, July 20, 1992)

67003815R00059